Lectionary Tales for the Pulpit

Series VII, Cycle B

for the Revised Common Lectionary

A Compendium of Stories from
StoryShare
a Component of **SermonSuite.com**
from CSS Publishing Company

CSS Publishing Company, Inc.
Lima, Ohio

LECTIONARY TALES FOR THE PULPIT

FIRST EDITION
Copyright © 2011
by CSS Publishing Co., Inc.

Published by CSS Publishing Company, Inc., Lima, Ohio 45807. All rights reserved. No part of this publication may be reproduced in any manner whatsoever without the prior permission of the publisher, except in the case of brief quotations embodied in critical articles and reviews. Inquiries should be addressed to: CSS Publishing Company, Inc., Permissions Department, 5450 N. Dixie Highway, Lima, Ohio 45807.

For more information about CSS Publishing Company resources, visit our website at www.csspub.com, email us at csr@csspub.com or call (800) 241-4056.

ISSN: 1938-7377

ISBN-13: 978-0-7880-2665-2
ISBN-10: 0-7880-2665-8   PRINTED IN USA

Table of Contents

Introduction   11

Advent 1   13
Mark 13:24-37
A Stellar Calamity

Advent 2   16
Mark 1:1-8
Overture

Advent 3   18
John 1:6-8, 19-28
The Gift of a John the Baptist

Advent 4   22
Luke 1:26-38; Psalm 89
The Jigsaw Puzzle

Christmas Eve / Christmas Day   25
Luke 2:1-14 (15-20)
Shepherds Camping in the Neighborhood

Christmas 1   28
Luke 2:22-40
The Promise

New Year's Day   31
Matthew 25:31-46
Conversation with a Madman

Epiphany of Our Lord   35
Matthew 2:1-12
The Chief Magi's Son

Baptism of Our Lord / Epiphany 1 / Ordinary Time 1   38
    Mark 1:4-11
    The Unexpected Tomorrow

Epiphany 2 / Ordinary Time 2   40
    1 Samuel 3:1-10
    It Can Happen Anywhere

Epiphany 3 / Ordinary Time 3   44
    Mark 1:14-20
    And They Followed Him?

Epiphany 4 / Ordinary Time 4   46
    Mark 1:21-28
    A Child of God

Epiphany 5 / Ordinary Time 5   49
    Mark 1:29-39
    Peter's Mother-in-Law

Epiphany 6 / Ordinary Time 6   52
    Mark 1:40-45
    The Deserving Recipient

Transfiguration of Our Lord   55
(Last Sunday after Epiphany)
    Mark 9:2-9; Psalm 50:1-6
    Listening

Ash Wednesday   58
    Joel 2:1-2, 12-17
    Sign of the Cross

Lent 1   60
Mark 1:9-15
Pain Is Generosity in Disguise

Lent 2   62
Mark 8:31-38; Psalm 22:23-31
Donkey Cross

Lent 3   64
Exodus 20:1-17
Traffic Control

Lent 4   66
Numbers 21:4-9
Sympathetic Magic

Lent 5   67
John 12:20-33
Showing Them Jesus

Passion / Palm Sunday   71
Mark 14:1—15:47
Holiday for Losers

Maundy Thursday   74
John 13:1-17, 31b-35
One More Passover

Good Friday   77
Isaiah 52:13—53:12
Healed by His Wounds

Easter Day   80
John 20:1-18
There Is No Death, Just Life

Easter 2   83
John 20:19-31
Doubt

Easter 3   87
Luke 24:36b-48
The Whole Truth

Easter 4   90
John 10:11-18; Psalm 23
The Goat Shepherd

Easter 5   93
John 15:1-8
Family Resemblance

Easter 6   95
John 15:9-17
The Roots of Love

Ascension of Our Lord   98
Luke 24:44-53
Witnessing to the Truth

Easter 7   101
Psalm 1; John 17:6-19
Choices

Pentecost Sunday   104
Acts 2:1-21
God's Spirit Changes Us

Holy Trinity Sunday   107
Isaiah 6:1-8
The Radiant Life

Proper 5 / Pentecost 2 / Ordinary Time 10 111
2 Corinthians 4:13—5:1
Marathon

Proper 6 / Pentecost 3 / Ordinary Time 11 116
Mark 4:26-34
The Kingdom of God Is Like This…

Proper 7 / Pentecost 4 / Ordinary Time 12 120
Mark 4:35-41
Passing Over to the Other Side

Proper 8 / Pentecost 5 / Ordinary Time 13 122
Psalm 130
A Deep Longing

Proper 9 / Pentecost 6 / Ordinary Time 14 124
Mark 6:1-13
Out in Faith

Proper 10 / Pentecost 7 / Ordinary Time 15 127
2 Samuel 6:1-5, 12b-19
Now That's Scary!

Proper 11 / Pentecost 8 / Ordinary Time 16 129
Mark 6:30-34, 53-56
Living with Pain

Proper 12 / Pentecost 9 / Ordinary Time 17 131
John 6:1-21
The Lad's Miracle of Sharing

Proper 13 / Pentecost 10 / Ordinary Time 18 133
Psalm 51:1-12; John 6:24-35
No Substitutes

Proper 14 / Pentecost 11 / Ordinary Time 19   136
  Psalm 130
  The Final Robert

Proper 15 / Pentecost 12 / Ordinary Time 20   139
  John 6:51-58
  Such a Deal!

Proper 16 / Pentecost 13 / Ordinary Time 21   141
  1 Kings 8:(1, 6, 10-11) 22-30, 41-43
  Solomon's Prayer

Proper 17 / Pentecost 14 / Ordinary Time 22   145
  Mark 7:1-8, 14-15, 21-23
  Curing Defilement

Proper 18 / Pentecost 15 / Ordinary Time 23   147
  Mark 7:24-37
  Harry Potter Lives

Proper 19 / Pentecost 16 / Ordinary Time 24   149
  Mark 8:27-38
  Questions, Answers, and the
  Difficulties of True Goodness

Proper 20 / Pentecost 17 / Ordinary Time 25   153
  Mark 9:30-37
  Five Days Old

Proper 21 / Pentecost 18 / Ordinary Time 26   156
  Mark 9:38-50
  Whoever Is Not Against Us…

Proper 22 / Pentecost 19 / Ordinary Time 27 158
   Mark 10:2-16
   "The Book"

Proper 23 / Pentecost 20 / Ordinary Time 28 162
   Mark 10:17-31
   Desperation's Opportunity

Proper 24 / Pentecost 21 / Ordinary Time 29 164
   Mark 10:35-45
   Achieving Greatness

Proper 25 / Pentecost 22 / Ordinary Time 30 168
   Job 42:1-6, 10-17; Hebrews 7:23-26
   Mistaken Identity

Reformation 171
   Jeremiah 31:31-34
   People with Chests

All Saints 173
   Revelation 21:1-6
   Strut Your Stuff

Proper 26 / Pentecost 23 / Ordinary Time 31 175
   Mark 12:28-34
   The Scribe

Proper 27 / Pentecost 24 / Ordinary Time 32 179
   Mark 12:38-44
   Giving All

Proper 28 / Pentecost 25 / Ordinary Time 33   182
Mark 13:1-8
A Stronger Foundation

Thanksgiving   185
Matthew 6:25-33
See?

Christ the King / Proper 29   187
Revelation 1:4b-8
Seeing the End

About the Authors   191

Introduction

Since you are reading this, you probably preach on a regular basis. It is important to not only bring God's word to the members of your congregation but to help make the gospel of Christ engaging and thought-provoking.

Most people know that Jesus, the Master Storyteller, very often used stories and parables to make an important point to his listeners about God's kingdom. Following his example, we know that helping people to understand God's word through the telling of a story not only provides additional interest in a message, but also makes that same message easier to understand.

Over the years, CSS has published thousands of relevant, interesting, and inspiring anecdotes and stories to season a pastor's sermon. Not only has CSS produced numerous books to aid pastors in this important part of ministry but CSS also has a weekly online service called **StoryShare**, a component of **SermonSuite.com**, that was created to bring preachers the most timely and relevant illustrations possible. This edition of stories and anecdotes, gleaned from **StoryShare** for Cycle B, are written to dovetail with the readings from the Revised Common Lectionary and will serve you well as extended illustrations or in many cases, stand alone sermons.

It is our hope that the stories in this book will not only assist you, the pastor, in your preaching but will also help you throughout your ministry.

The editors at CSS Publishing Company, Inc.

Advent 1
Mark 13:24-37
by Frank Ramirez

A Stellar Calamity

They say there's no use crying over spilled milk but how about over lost milk? Our word for "galaxy" comes from the Greek for "milk" — *galactos*. When they looked up in the sky and saw our Milky Way galaxy, they thought it looked like spilled milk that had spread across the sky. The Milky Way was so bright that on a moonless night it cast shadows! Nowadays even those of us who live in the countryside have trouble picking it out. And most Americans simply can't see it at all.

When Jesus talked about drastic changes in the sun, moon, and stars, he was speaking to people for whom they were reliable companions in the night sky. The psalmist said that the heavens declared the glory of God — yet now the heavens barely whisper to us. There is simply too much light pollution throughout much of our region of the world.

Sometimes it's not a matter of how bright a light is but how efficient. Billions of dollars are wasted by lights that illuminate the sky but not the property that people seek to protect at night. Lamps that are mounted on poles, for instance, actually create more darkness and insecurity because the structure casts a very dark shadow that can hide danger rather than reveal it!

Some areas are trying to use smarter lights to provide the illumination necessary for safety's sake — at least in our own mind — and not interfere with telescopes. For instance, San Jose requires the use of low-pressure streetlights to help Lick Observatory, which is nearby. In Tucson, as well as in other Arizona cities, there are ordinances that require outdoor lights using limited wavelengths that can be filtered out by telescopes and are pointed at the ground rather than at the sky. Pointing lights at the ground actually provides more security because any individuals or objects that might be dangerous are directly illuminated! Smart lights are saving cities a lot of money. In the case of the province of Alberta, Canada, the savings amounted to two million dollars a year.

Another problem is simply a matter of sleep. God has tied us to a cycle of waking and sleeping that is triggered by light and dark. We are out of sorts with the way God has created us. We don't know if we are coming or going. In some places the lights are so bright that people are forced to buy extra thick curtains because otherwise it never gets dark. Think of how sleepy everyone seems. No one seems to catch up. Are we really experiencing the night God has blessed us with?

No one is totally sure what effect this is having on the natural world. It has been discovered that light pollution is confusing migrating birds. Sometimes thousands can be killed in a single night. When the birds are gone, then the insects they would have eaten flourish and destroy forests and houses. In Florida the hatchlings of sea turtles emerge when it is night and instinctively head for the brightest light, which ought to be the moon. Instead, they are attracted by headlights and shopping centers, causing many of them to be run over.

The night sky told a story to ancient people all over the world. It was a living presence. Jesus used the images of the destruction of the night sky to symbolize the end of the world. Yet the night sky is not real to us. Nor are many of the other elements of Jesus' world — the strong smells of the unguents and perfumes, the kisses and embracing that bound people together, the hospitality that welcomed unexpected guests (requiring the host to knock on a neighbor's door at midnight for bread), the celebratory wedding feasts that included everyone in a town and not just selected guests, the openness of lives — all that has been banished by bright lights, obsessive privacy, suspicion of the unexpected, exclusivity, and a feeling that there is simply not enough to go around.

How can we pay attention to the signs that God is giving if we can't even see them? Have we put ourselves on the throne of the cosmos, creating a self-centered idolatry, losing not only the beauty of the natural world, including the night, but deposing God from the center of creation (in our own minds of course, and not in fact)? Have we not called into being the very Abomination of Desolation, which Jesus preached against in this passage?

Advent 2
Mark 1:1-8
by Keith Hewitt

Overture

I am not a student of music or theatre. For me, the day the music died came at age eight when a frustrated piano teacher told my parents to save their money — and it died again a few years later when I tried out for glee club in fifth grade and was given the job of keeping attendance at the practices — silently. My theatrical experience as a student was little better, consisting of one politically incorrect turn as "Silent Buffalo" in a play called *The Girl and the Gold Mine* or something like that. I was in ninth grade and learned a valuable lesson about the durability of incorrectly applied makeup. (I had "copper colored" skin for days after the curtain went down on Silent Buffalo.)

I say all of the above to let you know that I am not writing out of any scholarly understanding of music or theatre but from a layman's perspective. I believe what I say is correct… but am ready to stand corrected if it is not.

Apart from not wanting to be one of those clowns who is slipping in in front of everybody after a show has started — not to mention wanting to make sure you get your money's worth — there is one excellent reason to be waiting in your seat before the curtain ever goes up: to hear the overture.

An overture can be beautiful and moving as a stand-alone piece of music but it is more than that. It sets the tone for the show before the curtain ever rises. It contains, woven within it, many threads of music that you will hear throughout the show as distinctive melodies rise up, linger long enough to be identified, and then submerge back into it. In its progression of themes and rhythm, a well-written overture will foreshadow the rise and fall of the storyline. It is both a preview of the play to come and an encapsulation of the high points.

The audience, sitting in their seats waiting for the curtain to rise, is like the people of Israel thousands of years ago, waiting for the fulfillment of God's promise to them. After centuries of waiting, 2,000 years ago the lights dimmed and then the overture began, in the form of John the Baptist.

No simple holy man, no mad prophet, but a foreshadowing of the Savior to come and of his message. The ministry of John the Baptist was nothing less than an overture to the operatic passion of his cousin. The themes of rebirth and redemption would be played softly, to build anticipation for the words of Jesus. The call to turn away from the ways of the world would begin with John, and find its rhythm with the Messiah. His denial of self for the sake of service to a higher calling would be repeated and strengthened in the teachings of Jesus, and even his death would serve as a grim fore-echo of Jesus' death on Calvary.

The life and ministry of John the Baptist was an overture to the main event, and I wonder now… what part is my life playing in the drama of God's promise?

And am I playing the right tune?

Advent 3
John 1:6-8, 19-28
by David O. Bales

The Gift of a John the Baptist

"Did everyone read through your dozen resumés this week?" Pat Ochsner asked the rest of the Associate Pastor Nominating Committee. The eight others nodded.

"Well, you know the drill. You don't have to explain why you instantly reject a resumé. Flip them over here on the to-be-shredded heap." The members handed around stacks of resumés to one another and into the pile at Pat's end of the church library table. "Now, let's go to your one and two picks," Pat said, and the group did, reporting names of applicants, education, and experience.

The group spent a routine half-hour until Lewis said, "You know what, Pat? We're not into it tonight. All these bright people to be considered as associate pastor, yet I don't feel a spark in any of us about what we've read."

"I hadn't really noticed," Maxine spoke up. "But it's true." She looked to the chairperson, Pat, who was, along with everyone else, looking rather blank.

"I admit I've had a hard time concentrating," Gus said. Pat looked slowly around the large table, which was now littered with resumés. Everyone stared back at her.

"What is it?" she asked. "The weather?"

"I'm distracted," Tracey said. "I can't stop thinking about one woman and what she wrote. It was so strange. I didn't discard it, but she's not in my top two."

Gus bent toward Tracey and asked, "Who?"

"Judith Williams."

Gus slapped the table. "Same with me."

Lewis smiled, "I was intrigued, too."

Within a minute, everyone was smiling with relief. "Okay," Pat said, "let's look at her. Tracey, will you read the part of her resumé that's got you thinking? We'll all follow along. Everyone dig out Judith Williams' papers. What page? Three. All right."

Tracey read:

Dear Friends,

In asking for consideration to be called as your associate pastor, I want first to state that I'm not a pied piper. If you want someone to come solve your problems, it's not I. I'm disappointed in churches that hire paid staff to come do the congregation's work. I truly believe in the priesthood of all believers, whether anyone else does or not. I know plenty of pastors who say they do, yet whose style of leadership betrays not the slightest concern for the gifts of the laity. As a Labrador Retriever is genetically predisposed to run after something, grab it, and bring it back, so I am genetically predisposed to be an associate pastor.

I didn't learn this all at once. Like many women right out of seminary, I basically had two choices: be a small church pastor or an associate. In my case, being an associate chose me; however, I served as an associate the way most associates do — waiting for the chance to be head of staff.

I served under a head of staff who was, wonder of wonders, a woman: Alexandra Bracken. I wanted to be like her. So after four years I sought another call as solo pastor, and a church called me. I won't go into the details, but in the next three years I realized that I am hard-wired to be an associate. That's not second-rate nor is it a personality deficiency. As I identified the gifts and abilities of the lay people I ministered to, I began to better identify my own. My conclusion: I need to work on a team. It's not only helpful but downright necessary to have those, like John the Baptist, who point to the ministry of another, who with enthusiasm support someone else's ministry.

Let someone else design the dress — I'll sew it and enjoy doing it. Or, as my brother would say, someone else can carry the football — I'll block and not complain about it. In God's orchestra second fiddle is fine to play because that's the harmony.

Again, this isn't an awareness I came upon quickly or easily. But now I know, after having been an associate for more than twenty years, that such is the kind of position God calls me to, because such are the gifts and temperament God has given me. Thus, I offer my resumé for your consideration.

Sincerely,
Judith Williams

Tracey put down the resumé and smiled. "I like her and I want to talk more with her."

Lewis said, "I've been mulling her introductory letter all day."

"Pat," Gus said, "why don't we go ahead and contact Judith Williams now? I'm not saying she's the one God would have for us but she's certainly the kind of person I think we need."

Four months later, at a wonderful worship service on a Sunday evening, the congregation celebrated the call of their new associate pastor: Leonard Gutierrez. The next day the Associate Pastor Nominating Committee met for the last time. Because their work was done in confidentiality, they needed to hand in all notes and written material to be shredded.

Gus turned to Tracey and said, "Here's Judy Williams' resumé. Feels kind of sacred."

Tracey replied, "Exactly."

The committee members smiled to one another. Because of the confidentiality, they would never tell anyone that their new associate pastor listed The Reverend Judith Williams as a professional reference. But even if they could tell others about the extraordinary Judy Williams, only those with the gift of a John the Baptist would understand.

Advent 4
Luke 1:26-38; Psalm 89
by Argile Smith

The Jigsaw Puzzle

Laura and her grandmother Nan had been working on the jigsaw puzzle for days. Ever since Laura was old enough to comprehend the challenges of assembling a jigsaw puzzle, she and her grandmother had been working on them together. They shared a common passion for taking the little pieces of strangely cut cardboard and placing each of them in just the right place in order to produce a picture. And, of course, they shared the satisfaction that they had finished a daunting project together, which was always the best part of the entire effort.

As they got better at their joint effort, they came to measure the difficulty of the jigsaw puzzle by the number of pieces in the box and the scene to be reconstructed. Sometimes the scene made the puzzle easy to put together. That's why they really didn't prefer the easy puzzles. They liked the hard-to-figure-out scenes. So far, their favorite scene had been an autumn scene with a covered bridge in the center.

A couple of weeks before the Thanksgiving holiday, Nan found a puzzle at a yard sale that caught her eye. She knew that it would present a huge challenge for her and Laura, but not just because it contained 2,000 pieces. The scene had lots of blue sky with sparse clouds that displayed subtle hues of white and gray mixed together against the mammoth backdrop of various versions of blue. The sky reflected its colors in a mountain lake that covered the bottom of the scene. A thin horizon graced only with a few trees and hills separated the sky from the lake.

Nan knew that she had to have it for yet another reason: the box already had been opened. She didn't know for sure if all of the pieces of the puzzle were actually in the box. Just for good measure, the assurance of the high degree of difficulty was confirmed by a statement that the previous owner made after Nan purchased it. "Good luck on putting that thing together," she said with a note of warning. "I tried for weeks but didn't get anywhere."

She told Laura about the puzzle she had found and soon the two of them got started on it. They quickly found out that it proved to be just as difficult as Nan had anticipated. Days passed without any sure signs of progress. The music on the radio in Nan's living room had changed from instrumental favorites to Christmas classics before any significant progress could be noticed by either of them.

Listening to the music helped both of them to focus on their work. But one day it distracted Laura as she made another futile attempt at pushing a piece of the puzzle into place so the border of the puzzle would be completed. The song on the radio was "O Little Town of Bethlehem," and the words in the song had gotten next to her.

So she asked Nan, "What's the big deal about Bethlehem and baby Jesus? The whole story sounds like a fairy tale to me."

Nan replied, "You don't think that Jesus was born in Bethlehem?"

"Yes, I think he was, but it's all so random. I mean, out of nowhere a baby was born to a girl who had never — you know — and someone said he was God's Son. It's a nice story and all but I just don't get it."

"I see your point," Nan said. "But actually it was far more than a random act. For generations God had told his people that he would send his Messiah. You can see here and there in the Old Testament little bits and pieces of his promise. When the angel talked to Mary about Jesus' birth, he helped her to see that she would give birth to the Messiah God promised."

Nan went further in her explanation. "You see, it's a lot like this jigsaw puzzle. Some of the pieces don't seem to fit and we can't yet figure out how it's going to turn out. But one day the pieces will fall into place and we will get the full picture."

The psalmist hinted at the arrival of the Messiah (Psalm 89), and the angel promised Mary that it would happen (Luke 1:26-38). Advent gives us a chance to see the scene of redemption after all of the pieces have been placed in the puzzle.

Christmas Eve / Christmas Day
Luke 2:1-14 (15-20)
by Sandra Herrmann

Shepherds Camping in the Neighborhood

I love the way Eugene Peterson phrases the situation of the shepherds: "There were sheepherders camping in the neighborhood. They had set night watches over their sheep." It puts their situation in terms many of us understand — the difficulties of camping out.

In my young adulthood, my husband and I loved to camp. In fact, our honeymoon was an entire summer between college graduation and the start of graduate school. We had never been camping before but we decided this was the way we wanted to spend the twelve weeks available. So off we went to learn what we would need: a 10' x 12' cottage-style tent; two air mattresses; two sleeping bags that could also be zipped together for cozy evenings; a camp stove with all the requisite pots, pans, and utensils; a lantern; a large hard-sided cooler with a locking top (in case of bears, raccoons, and other wildlife used to foraging from humans); plates, as well as knives, forks, and spoons; and some good hiking boots. When we had all that, we packed up and headed for the woods.

What I was not prepared for was how difficult it is to keep clean when you're camping. Oh yes, there are shower rooms, a bit shaggy from the constant use, but we had to go to the pump to get drinking water and had to heat water on the stove to do the dishes. And those shower rooms are often cold, so you have to be brave to take off your clothes and step under the water, not to mention drying off afterward.

Then there are the vagaries of weather. At one point, we seemed to be crossing Canada at precisely the same rate as a rather nasty thunderstorm we had picked up in Nova Scotia. For a week we had to fold up a wet tent and load everything into the trailer in varying states of wetness. By the end of the week, the tent smelled a bit dank. So did we. Happily, in twentieth-century Canada we could (at last!) pull into a laundromat and see to it that everything was clean and dry. And since I had had all the fun I could take for a while, we could also rent a room, sleep on a real bed, and stand under a shower that never ran out of hot water.

That was not the case with the shepherds of Jesus' day. There was no hot water unless you built a fire. No shower stalls, fluffy towels, or aromatic shampoos. No dryer to see to it that your clothes were both dry and smelling fresh. And that's not to mention the sheep they slept next to! The lanolin in their wool keeps their skin fairly dry but wet wool on the hoof has a pungent odor not to be forgotten.

In short, the shepherd's life was not a clean one. There were times when they might camp near a quiet river (sheep are terrified of fast-running water). Then they would put up their tents and spread carpets on the ground, sometimes in layers to cushion them from rocks and clots of clay. Then they might have the opportunity to bathe.

But most likely, the shepherds who showed up at the cave where Mary and Joseph and the baby were sheltered smelled of the wood of their campfires and the garlic with which they seasoned their simple evening meal. Their clothes probably bore the rents and tears from thorn trees in which sheep are easily caught as they graze, not to mention the cockleburs that would adhere to the hems of their robes as they walked along. Probably there were muddy stains from the riverbank and spots from where they accidently dropped a bite or two of food on their clothes. And there would be the earthy, even musky, smell of the sheep. All of these smells would be a normal part of life to those who sleep in tents or caves most nights of the year.

Add to that the fact that most shepherds were boys in the age range of eight to fourteen. There might be two or three grown men (20-25) to circulate around the sleepy herds but most of the shepherding was done by boys. Past that age, most boys would be apprenticed out. Some would learn how to shear sheep and clean the wool for sale. Others would learn how to do the butchering, both to eat and to sell at market. The hardest, muddiest, dirtiest part of making a living with the family herd was left to the boys who had to learn how to fend off wild dogs and wolves and the various other dangers that threaten disaster for your sheep.

So here came the shepherds — the dirty, curious, feisty, street-smart kids who minded the sheep, but for whom the invitation of the angels was a powerful draw... leaving the sheep in a cave or stone circle, watched by someone who had to be mature enough to be left behind when this magical event of meeting angels took place. Here they came, pushing and shoving for a glimpse of a baby who is Messiah, the Lord. Here they were, the dirty, the childish, the curious, pushing each other to get to see a girl not much older than they were nursing her baby. What a motley crew. What a choice God made, sending a personal invitation by messengers from heaven to this bunch.

Christmas 1
Luke 2:22-40
by Craig Kelly

The Promise

"Another coffee, Joe?"

"No thanks, Gail, I'm good for now."

Gail brushed a lock of auburn hair tinged with gray out of her face, tucking it behind her ear. She smiled and nodded before she continued to check on other patrons. She had been working at that diner for twenty years. She knew the routine.

The old man had been sitting at his usual table next to the front door of the all-night diner. It was the same every New Year's Eve. He would arrive promptly at 8 p.m., dressed in a black double-breasted suit, pressed white shirt, shined dress shoes, and red tie. He would be clutching a long cardboard box to his chest as he walked in out of the cold, and every year that box would be carrying one red carnation. He would take his seat, set his box aside, and order a coffee, black.

And then he would wait.

Every night as patrons would come in and toast the end of the old year and the beginning of the new, Joe would sit, watching the door, waiting for that one face, the one he never saw. He would sigh heavily, crestfallen as the crowd in the diner watched the ball drop on the television over the bar, joining in the countdown. Once midnight would come, he would slowly put on his coat and hat, remove the carnation from the box, and go home, leaving the carnation and three dollars on the table for payment and tip.

It had been the same scene every New Year's Eve for too many years.

It was 1952, and Joe had just been released after being held by the North Koreans as a POW. Before returning to the States, he sent his fiancée a letter:

My dear May,
I'd just come back from another bombing run when I got the news: I'm coming home! It probably won't be until just after Christmas, but I should be there by New Year's Eve.
I know it's been hard for you to wait for me these past two years, not knowing if I'd be dead or alive, but I want you to know how much coming home to you has meant to me, and now that it's happening, I can't really believe it!
I'll be at Mac's Diner on 11th Street on New Year's Eve at 8:00. I'll be waiting there for you.
I love you.
Joe

The night of December 31, 1952, came — and sure enough Joe was there, dressed in a black double-breasted suit, pressed white shirt, shined dress shoes, and red tie. He clutched a long cardboard box to his chest as he came in out of the cold, protecting the red carnation that was inside. He sat at the table next to the front door, ordered a coffee, black, and waited.

When May never came, Joe asked around, only to discover that she had given him up for dead and moved out of state. Mutual friends would tell him, "Just let it go, Joe. She's got a new life now. Move on." And every time, Joe would reply, "I made a promise to her. I would wait for her at Mac's. If you see her, tell her I'm going to keep my word and I'll be there waiting for her."

And every year Joe would be there, and every year Joe would leave disappointed right after midnight. And every year Joe would come back.

When Gail finished checking on the other customers, she came back to Joe's table, set the coffee pot down, and sat across from him.

"Hey, Joe, do you mind if I ask you a question?"

Joe looked up from his coffee mug. "Not at all, Gail. What would you like to know?"

She leaned in. "I know why you're here. I heard about May and what she did to you. What I want to know is why you keep coming. Why do you put yourself through this every year, only to leave every year disappointed? May's obviously moved on, hun. Why don't you? It's been over fifty years."

Joe sighed. "It's simple, Gail. I promised her I would wait here for her and I don't want to make a liar of myself when she does show up. In my heart, I know she's out there, and I wouldn't be true to myself if I gave up on her. When she comes through that door I'll be here, with a smile on my face and a carnation in my hand." He looked down at his coffee mug. "You know, maybe I could use a warm-up after all."

Gail shook her head, smiled, and refilled his mug.

New Year's Day
Matthew 25:31-46
by Keith Hewitt

Conversation with a Madman

The room was bathed in fluorescent light, almost intense enough to be uncomfortable — not the intent, he suspected, but just a side benefit. The fixtures, behind sturdy cages, emitted a low hum that hovered at the edge of hearing, like a ghost seen only out of the corner of one's eye. He had spent too much time after his first visit trying to figure out what the noise was on his digital recorder. Then he had asked about moving somewhere else in the room, out from under the fixtures — and had been told "No," in no uncertain terms.

Any interviews needed to be conducted in the stark fluorescent light, in full view of the observers. Anything else, they explained, would not be safe.

So he turned on the recorder, glanced at the red LED that told him it was running, and set it on the table, then slid it carefully across the pale green formica until it was directly in front of the subject. "Allan Randolph Stone," he said crisply, "December 29." He paused and looked at his watch. "Approximately 34 hours before his scheduled execution."

He leaned back, set his arms on the table, folded his hands, and studied the man before him. Stone was a spare man with clear blue eyes and crewcut hair the color of hot charcoal. His skin was pale, his hands and face soft, and the way the orange jumpsuit hung on him made it clear that he had not spent his years bulking up in the exercise yard.

He looked like anybody's grandfather. It was hard to reconcile that with the murders that had brought him to this place.

"How does it feel, knowing that you're going to die?" he asked the man across the table from him.

"I don't know," Stone answered and spread his manacled hands. "You tell me."

"What do you mean?"

"You tell me what it's like, knowing you're going to die. Unless you're not going to. Do you have some arrangement with God the rest of us don't?"

He folded his arms and frowned. "You know what I mean."

"I know exactly what you mean. And your question tells me that you haven't thought about the truth here."

"What truth would that be?"

"You tell me."

The lights hummed softly in the silence, and he frowned. The pointlessness of the exchange was irritating him. "If you don't want to talk, why did you agree to the interview?"

"I am more than willing to talk, young man. But I want to talk about important things. The time for trivia is past... long past."

"What's trivial about wanting to know how it feels to know that you're going to die in a day and a half?"

"Ah, now that's a different question." Stone leaned forward and smiled slightly. "I feel lucky."

"Lucky?"

"I do. I feel lucky." He paused for a moment or two, time enough for a couple of heartbeats — and he felt them within, knowing that two more beats had fallen off the finite list of heartbeats left to him. "Most people — you, for instance — live your life as though you're not going to die. Oh sure, intellectually you can mouth the words — but deep inside, where it counts, where you believe it, you don't really think so. It's somewhere off in the mists of maybe, like winning the lottery or aliens landing on the White House lawn."

"So how does that make you lucky?"

"Having a date certain when somebody is going to do me the favor of stopping my heart — it focused me. It gave me the motivation to get right with God, in a way nothing else could do. Not for me, anyway. All the preaching in the world, all the Sunday school teachers and pastors you could line up from here to eternity couldn't touch me as much as someone in the Circuit Court circling a date on the calendar and saying, 'you go this far, and no further.' "

"So you've been 'saved'? A jailhouse conversion?"

"Does that cheapen it? Tell me, if you go to a doctor who tells you that you've got high cholesterol and you've got to follow a certain strict diet or die… if your doctor tells you that, and you change your attitude and your diet, is it any less healthy, or any less meaningful, than if you had discovered healthy eating on your own?"

The visitor frowned. "I'm not sure that's an equivalent situation."

"It's exactly equivalent from my standpoint. You read about judgment day and it's an interesting story… I read about it and for me it's the reality of the day after tomorrow. You have the sad luxury of a bucket of sand that you can bury your head in. The court took mine away the day they set an execution date. And I've sent the judge a thank-you note for that."

"Really?"

"Really." Stone inched around in his seat and as his eyebrows drew together his eyes grew veiled. "That doesn't mean it's all sunshine and roses. I feel badly — I feel badly for the people I… the people I killed…" He felt around for the right words, tested them before he set them out. "I took people away from their own journeys, their own lives, and I don't know where each of them stood with God. I wake up at night crying because I dreamed that one or the other of them had not found their way before I did what I did. And I feel badly because I put their friends and family in a place where it seemed reasonable to question God… and that's just not my place to do. I had no right, and I was wrong. That's what haunts me." The veil before him seemed to clear a bit then and he brightened. "But at least in another day or so I'll know — and it won't be haunting me anymore."

"I see." The lights hummed. "Is there anything else my readers should know?"

"Nothing you would understand. Or they, I'm afraid."

The visitor frowned, reached for the recorder, hesitated, and drew his hand back. "So you expect me to believe that you're okay with knowing that you're going to die the day after tomorrow?"

"Oh no," Stone answered quickly. "Did I give you that impression? I'm sorry. I don't expect you to believe that, anymore than I expect you to believe that you and I both live with the same cloud over our heads. In your mind, in your world, I'm the poor SOB who's living on borrowed time. And I know that. But what I know, and you don't, is that you are too. In 34 hours, someone's going to stick a needle in my vein and stop my heart. I've ordered my life around the fact that I'm going to die because my nose has been rubbed in that reality. How about you?"

"I don't plan on murdering anybody, so I've got time."

Stone smiled. "My point exactly." He leaned forward again and spread his manacled hands. "I'd really like to know how you're going to spin this — but I'm afraid I never will. I've got a prior engagement."

"I'll try to get a draft to you," the visitor promised, and turned off the recorder.

As he listened to the interview again that night, he stared at the blank monitor before him and knew he would not be getting that draft to Stone in time. But then again, he thought, promises to a madman could hardly be binding.

And in his arm, a fleck of plaque peeled away from the vein wall, and began its journey toward his heart…

Epiphany of Our Lord
Matthew 2:1-12
by David O. Bales

The Chief Magi's Son

The chief magi's son had never wanted to leave Persia and go off after a star; and during the weeks on the journey, if anyone would listen to him, he'd try to make them understand, "Stars shine everywhere." His magi companions habitually smiled at his contrariness. His father, the chief magi, endured his questions even when they bordered more on blasphemy than interrogation: "Look at the sky. Has it changed since we left three months ago?" His father, no matter how difficult the road or how hot the day, habitually said, "You'll see." When that response didn't win his son over, the chief magi would just smile and pat him on the shoulder.

Now they'd gone through the mockery of an interview with Herod. The chief magi's son felt the hair on his neck prickle when Herod displayed his oily smile. Did they really think this tyrant was pleased that a rival king was born outside his dynastic line? As they were escorted from Herod's audience room he whispered to two magi, "Don't you see that Herod is suspicious?" But since he'd been such a consistent nag for months, the magi smiled gently and made their preparations to continue toward Bethlehem. Truly, the chief magi's son didn't try as hard to convince them anymore. No matter their expectations for his also becoming a magi, he'd only come along because he'd promised his mother to watch out for his father, and their patience with him had nearly worn him down.

Only once more did he try to convince his father that they were putting their heads in the lion's mouth. His father replied, "Yes, the Lion of the tribe of Judah." His father shushed his son, "We're almost there." He patted his son on the shoulder. "Another morning's travel. You'll see."

The next morning they left Jerusalem — camels, donkeys, attendants, and magi. The chief magi's son made sure he was last. He glanced back toward Jerusalem and saw Herod's men atop the city wall watching them. He expected to see them again soon.

What had captured the minds of these Zoroastrian priests, who until a year ago had seemed so reasonable, so stable, even staid? The dangerous pilgrimage to Judea was only one thing. To think that a star could guide them anywhere was at least foolish and bordered on self-destruction. Didn't they realize you can see a star from anywhere? That's one large sky up there, seen from all points on earth. Stars don't stand over anything. Stars move all night and all year.

The caravan arrived in Bethlehem at midday. Their entourage with their foreign clothes and strange dialect upset the villagers. The magi announced that they'd come seeking the child born King of the Jews and Messiah. The chief magi's son sighed and said to a boy holding a camel's bridle, "Why don't we just return to Jerusalem and turn ourselves in for sedition?" Herod would act swiftly if even one village sprouted hope for a different king.

No one in Bethlehem knew of a special baby, although the magi made a number of young mothers happy by their visits. In the late afternoon the magi gathered for a council and determined they must wait for nightfall and the star to direct them. The chief magi's son sat beyond their circle and remained silent during the discussion.

That evening as the stars appeared the old men, professional astrologers, stood gazing at the heavens, identifying constellations. One said, "There it is." The others shouted agreement. Then they ran, grabbing gifts they'd carted for a hundred days. Adorned in their Persian priestly garb, the old men dashed through the dark street like frail birds flying at night. The chief magi's son followed in order to pick up any who fell. He didn't want them hurt. Who else would have put up with him as they did? He was already planning a way home for them by some route other than through Herod's Jerusalem.

Ahead of him his father kept looking up at the stars, then down to see the dark, irregular alley. He stopped and pointed to the house that he said the star shined over. His son looked up also, seeing all stars shining over all houses. The men knocked and were welcomed in. They entered in such joy they didn't realize that the chief magi's son stayed outside.

He'd gotten his father safe halfway. He'd promised his mother he'd also usher him home safely. Alone in Bethlehem's dark street, away from the old men's excitement, the chief magi's son looked up quietly and said, "God, I don't know whose child they've come upon. But they're good men full of hopes. They're old men consumed with dreams. They're not like so many people who've been hollowed out by life. These men, led by my father, are looking for something extraordinary — not for their own benefit. They aren't seeking you in order to become rich and powerful.

"Great Creator, if you reward anyone for faithfulness, look upon them, I pray. They follow their abnormal star, which they think shines only here. Grant them some touch upon this earth of life beyond. Don't let their waning years be filled with regret. Bestow upon them, I pray, satisfaction with a quest that grows in mercy and kindness and that spreads to others as goodwill.

"Merciful and Almighty, if I also must become a priest, I ask that you impart to me a portion of their faith and compassion, for these are the best men I've ever known. And if I, as they expect, must serve an earthly Messiah, may he be as hopeful as these magi and as good as my father.

"In hope for the world I pray. Amen."

Baptism of Our Lord / Epiphany 1 / Ordinary Time 1
Mark 1:4-11
by Peter Andrew Smith

The Unexpected Tomorrow

"I'm not staying on as your minister," Ralph said firmly.

"Pastor," the Chair of the Board said, "I know we haven't always seen eye to eye but for the good of the congregation I'd be willing to make things work."

Ralph smiled. "My leaving has nothing to do with you disagreeing with me. You're a good man who loves God and his church. We just have different ways of doing things."

The Chair of the Board shook his head. "Then I don't understand — if it's not me, then why won't you stay? There is a good feeling in the congregation after years of us fighting with each other. There is a growing crowd on Sunday morning and our finances mean we can consider hiring that youth pastor we've always wanted. Our congregation is poised to explode with new people and new programs. We just have to make sure we have the right man leading us to keep things going this way."

"And that is exactly why I am leaving," Ralph said. "You need the right person to lead you and I am not that person."

"How could you not be that person? You were the lone voice who came and took the broken parts of this church and called us back to God. You refused to let us continue hurting each other and demanded that we be Christians in more than just name. We've done those things and are enjoying the renewed prosperity of this church."

"Yes, you have done all those things — which is why I am leaving. Because God brought me here to prepare the way and that's what I have done. And now the next person will be coming."

"Next person?"

"The one God is sending to set this place on fire with the Holy Spirit. You're ready spiritually, emotionally, and financially for the next great thing God has planned for you. When the person arrives to lead you, then things will happen which I cannot even imagine."

The Chair of the Board looked shocked. "But you know us. You've brought us so far — how can you not know where we are headed?"

Ralph put his hand on the man's shoulder. "Because I'm not the person God wants to do that work with you. That is for the next pastor who will preach and serve among you."

The Chair shrugged. "I still think you're the man to lead us but I know better than to argue with you when your mind is made up. Do you suppose the next pastor will be a man like you?"

Ralph shrugged. "I have no idea. She might be younger or she might be older."

The Chair of the Board's mouth hung open as he walked away. Ralph felt a wave of satisfaction in having planted the last seed he needed to in order to finish the work God had called him to do with the congregation.

Epiphany 2 / Ordinary Time 2
1 Samuel 3:1-10
by John Smylie

It Can Happen Anywhere

It was going to be a very long day. Three flights from the East Coast to the West. The first leg would depart Sarasota in the early afternoon, arriving in Atlanta, Georgia, a few hours later. After a several-hour layover, the second leg would leave Atlanta on its way to Minneapolis-St. Paul. The third and final leg of the journey would bring the traveler into Casper, Wyoming, a little past 11 p.m. Mountain Time.

The traveler was tall and he wasn't looking forward to the cramped seating found in the coach seats in the airlines. His 6'3" frame just simply didn't fit, and the problem was that he could not get assigned seats before his flight. He learned over the years to ask for an exit row and most of the time he was successful in getting one but recently he discovered the airlines were asking for more money for the extra inches. He felt the tickets were already overpriced, perhaps because the flights originated from smaller markets. His current ticket was $778 round-trip and he felt that was quite enough.

On the way down to Florida he found himself quite fortunate. On all three of his legs he received his request of an exit row at no extra charge. In fact, on December 26 there were not many people flying on the airplane (at least it wasn't overcrowded), and on one of the legs he was actually the only person sitting in the exit row. But today was January 1 and travelers were on the move. Even though it was a holiday it seemed like many people wanted to beat the weekend rush that a few days later would bring.

He walked up to the counter in Sarasota and made his request to the Delta Airlines agent, who looked him up and down and saw how difficult it would be for him to fit in the center seat. Perhaps it was compassion on her part, or the fact that he asked her how she was feeling (for she looked as if she might be a bit hungover) that caused her to have mercy and assign him to an exit row. On the second leg of his journey home, this time on Northwest Airlines, he once again received the mercy of the agent, who assigned him to an aisle seat exit row. In fact, the agent in Atlanta assigned him to an exit row on the little fifty-passenger jet that flies between Minneapolis-St. Paul and Casper, Wyoming. He had about an hour and 45 minutes before the plane was to leave. Minneapolis-St. Paul is a very large airport, and he wandered from one side of the airport, where his plane landed, to the other, where his next plane would depart. He made himself comfortable as he sat down and sought to finish the book he started at the beginning of his journey.

The Shack had been an easy read and because he was a minister himself most of the theological challenges within the book were things he'd already thought about. But he felt it was important to read the book, as many in his congregation had been talking about it. It pointed them toward radical forgiveness and a better understanding of the Trinity; at least that's what he heard from them. He found himself somewhat disturbed by the book, especially the part about the little child. While he was in the airport he kept looking at children who seemed so vulnerable to him. He was bothered that the book might give some folks ideas that could be used to hurt children.

While he was in Minneapolis at his gate area waiting for the airplane first to arrive and then to load and depart, he noticed a particularly large man. It was hard to miss this gentleman because he must've weighed around 400 pounds. He also appeared as if he hadn't washed for a week. Under his breath and in the silence of reading his book the traveler said to himself and whoever else might be listening to his thoughts, "Please don't let me sit next to this person." He knew that the two of them would never fit in the seats. The flight was on time for boarding and because he had an exit row he was invited to go in a bit early to become familiar with the exit procedures in the event of an emergency. The plane was full and he watched as the passengers came down the narrow aisle. Before long the large man was on his way, and our traveler knew immediately who he was going to be sitting next to. Sure enough, he stood at the end of the two seats, showed his ticket and our traveler stepped out so the large man could slide into his window seat. In fact he fit into one and a half of the seats, so it was obviously going to be an uncomfortable two-plus hours — made longer because of icing conditions and the fact that the airplane needed to be de-iced before it would be released for takeoff.

"*Samuel! Samuel!*" *And he said, "Here I am!"*

Lord! Lord! "Were you listening to my thoughts, Lord?" our traveler wondered. His immediate response went in two directions after the large man found his seat. The first was being annoyed at having to ride with great discomfort for the next few hours — a somewhat selfish response. But then a few moments later or perhaps a few seconds later, he found himself wondering why God had brought this man to sit next to him, especially after his plea to be able to ride in a bit more comfort. *Traveler! Traveler! Come out of your own way of thinking, discover who it is who is talking to you, and break out of your own expectations and discover what I have for you.*

The overweight and unkempt man turned out to be very humble. He sat sideways and forward so as to take as little of our traveler's seat as he could. Our traveler was aware of his judgmental spirit. He was supposed to be a faithful Christian with the fruit of the Spirit growing within him — patience, kindness, gentleness — but the fruit was obviously in the overweight passenger who clearly hadn't had a shower for over a week. His posture indicated his humility, for he was very self-aware and was concerned that his great size was causing discomfort to the traveler.

Have you ever wondered, or discovered, how the Lord meets us? We think that moments like our Lord speaking to Samuel in the middle of the night are rare. But really they are all around us. Our Lord was speaking to our tall traveler before he got on the plane. Our Lord was preparing him to be humbled and to become aware of his own judgmental attitude. Once Samuel became aware that it was God who was speaking to him, he was able to know how to respond. I wonder how often the Lord is speaking to us, offering us an opportunity to respond in a way that will bring us blessings and growth and new life.

I know this traveler met God on this journey; I know he was humbled by God and by his own narrow attitude and thinking. I know this because I was the traveler, and my hunch is that if you look into your life, your journey, your attitudes, you will find opportunities when our Lord is seeking to break through the barriers you may have created around your heart and the protective layers that you put around your life, as I put around mine. The good news is that God cares enough to break through our sleep, our negative attitudes, our lack of respect, our limited perspectives, so that we can be awakened to his grace, mercy, and presence.

And Samuel said, "Speak, for your servant is listening."

Epiphany 3 / Ordinary Time 3
Mark 1:14-20
by C. David McKirachan

And They Followed Him?

When I was younger, I wondered why these people who became the apostles walked away from their jobs and their families so easily just because Jesus talked to them. Were they weak-minded? Would Jesus want people who could be that easily swayed? Did he hypnotize them? Was he into mind control? None of the simple answers explained away the problems I had with "… and they left their nets and followed him."

I'd heard sermons on the power of Jesus, on the presence of God that lit him and how people were attracted to him. But my problems just wouldn't recede with the "Jesus says jump and they said how high" approach to the call of these people who were so pivotal in the dawning of the new age. Jesus constantly demanded that they wrestle with their own issues, come to their own conclusions, and make choices from high ground. And he was more likely to tell them to "hoof it" than carry them there.

When I was thirteen, I went to church camp and had a very clear experience of salvation. I came home lit with the fire of God's love and proceeded to preach to my parents. I was devastated when they didn't praise God and fall on their knees. They told me they were happy and that this would be one of many milestones in my journey of faith. My devastation wore off. The experience and its importance still radiated the Holy Spirit's heat for me, but I realized I had a few more things to learn before I assumed it would all be downloaded at one pop. My parents' patience and unwavering willingness to be present in my life taught me more about God's call than any inspirational moment.

I have remembered that and endeavored to be a willing and patient presence in people's lives. The "patient" part gets rough sometimes. I want to do mind control on those idiots who don't agree with me. And it drives me nuts when they take a perfectly clear passage from scripture and run out into right or left field with it, proving again that left to their own they'll wander into hell. But then I remember that it's not my job to create puppets. If God didn't, why should I try?

So I wonder about this call-response thing. I wonder how they wrestled. I wonder what issues tore and scared them. I wonder about their hungers and their needs. I wonder about their wives and their children. And I keep coming back to that patient presence that refuses to let up on any of us. Yes, they gave up a lot. They probably fought battles in the middle of the night, battles of doubt and anxiety that we will never know about except by remembering our own battles. But the gravitational love of Christ somehow would not go away. And so they left their nets and their lives behind and journeyed with him.

But sometimes I still wish I could do mind control….

Epiphany 4 / Ordinary Time 4
Mark 1:21-28
by Frank Ramirez

A Child of God

Did you ever notice the irony of these verses — an irony that is repeated over and over again in the first eight chapters of Mark? God's people, his hometown, and even the friends of Jesus fail to recognize him for who he is. Even after Jesus stills the storm his disciples will ask, "Who then is this, that even the wind and the sea obey him?" (Mark 4:41).

But the sick, the possessed, the Gentiles, the outsiders all recognize Jesus. They name him.

I was familiar enough with the gospel of Mark that I was no longer surprised when it occurred in the pages of scripture — but that didn't stop me from being surprised when it happened in real life.

Each week I go to the local county jail to run a Bible study. I'm part of an ecumenical team of ministers who have been granted permission to be a daily part of prison life in our area. Each day the men and the women who are imprisoned have the option to go to a church service or Bible study, each run by a different minister. Though we come from many different denominations and backgrounds, we are a team.

Some of the church leaders have a well-designed program where they walk the prisoners through a passage and disseminate knowledge. I operate a little differently, opening my Bible where I left off last week and inviting prisoners to take turns reading a verse or two, and to respond with their own ideas after I say a few sentences about the passage. I encourage them to find applications for their lives but it never occurred to me to ask them to find applications for my life. I was there to give, after all, not receive.

I will call this inmate Paul, after the apostle. It is not his real name. I never asked inmates what crime they might have committed. If they wanted to, they told me. If not, I respected their privacy. Paul had said on more than one occasion that he'd lived a pretty sinful life.

He also said that even if he didn't necessarily deserve to go to jail for the crime the authorities claimed he committed, he had done plenty to earn time in jail, so he couldn't complain. Moreover, being in prison had caused him to open a Bible and read — then reread again and again — God's holy word. Paul moved freely from one text to another, making connections and sharing insights.

As it turned out I was planning to preach on Galatians 4:4-7, but found myself puzzled about where I should go. Normally sermon preparation is not a problem for me, but having chosen this text, I found I couldn't get a handle on it.

We were in the middle of the gospel of Mark, as I recall, during our weekly time together, when suddenly Paul said, "You know, this reminds me of what Paul wrote in Galatians 4:4-7." He then opened his Bible and read the passage:

> But when the fullness of time had come, God sent his Son, born of a woman, born under the law, in order to redeem those who were under the law, so that we might receive adoption as children. And because you are children, God has sent the Spirit of his Son into our hearts, crying, "Abba! Father!" So you are no longer a slave but a child, and if a child then also an heir, through God.

Paul (the prisoner) then proceeded to explain how outsiders, even prisoners, could become children of God, with the full rights of someone who was raised in the church. It had all been made possible by the love of God through Jesus. That meant, he explained, that even though he lived in prison and couldn't come and go as he pleased, he was no longer shackled like a slave but had become a child and heir of God. He went on to say he had come to recognize the hand of Jesus in his time in prison. He could proclaim Jesus as Son of God.

There it was — my sermon. Of course I gave Paul credit and explained the circumstances, and I reminded my parishioners how, in the gospel of Mark, the least likely easily recognized Jesus. Some of these might be tortured individuals like this possessed man, who needed Jesus to free him from his emotional prison.

Epiphany is the time we celebrate that outsiders like the magi, and others who we encounter in the gospels, will stop at nothing to proclaim and follow Jesus as Lord. The important thing for those of us who are fat and sassy in the pews, a little smug about how long we've been on God's team to the point we can no longer recognize the action of Jesus in our lives, is to keep our ears and eyes open, so we recognize what lengths Jesus will go to get our attention. And if we don't trust ourselves, trust the outsiders. They know better than us — Jesus is Lord!

Epiphany 5 / Ordinary Time 5
Mark 1:29-39
by David O. Bales

Peter's Mother-in-Law

"To start with, I don't mind if you call me Peter's mother-in-law," the old lady said. She spoke over her shoulder as she shuffled farther into her house. The seven visitors followed her and each gawked at a portion of a ripped fish net and a broken oar hanging on the wall. They waited for the lady of the house to slowly turn to them. "Not that I was always proud of the young man."

A man near her flinched and stepped back from her. The old lady, faster than seemed possible for her age, leaned toward him. "Something wrong with telling the truth?"

"Well," the man choked as he spoke, "you're talking about a leader in Jesus' church. I thought if we came to his house he'd be mentioned with more respect."

"Ha," the old lady teetered when she laughed, putting her hand behind her to brace herself against the wall. "Do you have a son-in-law?"

Her smile toward him was a continuing question. The man remained silent, but the woman with him, obviously his wife, sniggered.

"And don't you laugh about your relatives?" The man gave a foolish look but didn't dispute further with this tottery, ancient woman who had proven herself to be a wit but a benevolent one.

"I love Peter." She spoke to the whole group now. "None of you can probably say that. But here, let's all get comfortable." Everyone found places to sit facing her.

"Any of you ever met him? Well, if you'd grown up near Bethsaida or Capernaum, you'd have realized he was a pretty stubborn young man. Even though he knew his letters, that didn't mean he was truly educated or anywhere near mature. No one could tell him where to fish, even if he wasn't catching anything — except Jesus.

"I should know and I appreciate getting to tell you. Bilshan waits until he has a handful of curious visitors before he brings a group of you to see where Peter lived and have a chat about him. Fine to call me Peter's mother-in-law. I'm not only used to it, but I'm proud of it. However, don't call this Peter's house. It's mine.

"I suppose you'd like to know about that." She shifted on her cushion and grimaced as she got more comfortable. "When he married my daughter he moved here, even brought his brother Andrew. Makes sense. My husband — also a fisherman — had died three months before and the docks here are a lot better than at Bethsaida. Easier to unload their catch. But these rock walls were mine and Peter was welcome here. Most important to me was that he was good to my daughter who, by the way, doesn't mind being called Peter's wife.

"Now, the reason I don't mind being called Peter's mother-in-law and my daughter doesn't mind being called Peter's wife is that my son-in-law doesn't mind being called Jesus' disciple. It took a while for Peter to arrive at that — you remember his denying Jesus three times, but it came naturally to me. Only took me a moment to understand Jesus.

"Do you know that Jesus healed me? I was sick. Jesus had never been here before; yet he came to my pallet, took me by the hand, and lifted me up. Simple enough. I was healed. Now, the difference between me and my boneheaded son-in-law is that I understood Jesus instantly. I immediately began to serve him. Peter, however, and he'd tell you this himself, never quite got it until Jesus was resurrected. He took off with his brother and the two other fishermen, James and John. They followed Jesus. They came back when they were hungry or tired and worked a while, but basically my daughter and I were on our own. Peter was gone with Jesus. But no matter how much time Peter spent with Jesus, he was always expecting Jesus to do wonderful things for him. Many times I said to him, 'You serve him, Peter.' He always answered, 'I am, Mother, I am.' But I could never get through to him the difference between what he was saying and what we could all tell he expected of Jesus.

"I think this is the most joyous part of being Peter's mother-in-law. When a batch of you shows up here I get to tell you what Peter learned and what we all realized after Jesus' resurrection. Jesus was more than any of us thought. Jesus is God's heart visible.

"And you know what else I get to do? I get to tell you about that smelly old fish net and that broken oar. If they were serviceable I wouldn't have them. Now they're pegged to the wall just for you. Any ideas why they're there and what they mean?" The seven strangers stared at the wall and looked serious.

After a pause she laughed again. "They don't mean anything! I put them there just so they'd help visitors like you recognize this as a fisherman's house. The net and the oar are no more important than that Peter lived in this house or that I'm Peter's mother-in-law. Jesus is important. Peter understands that now. My daughter understands that. Those two travel serving Jesus."

She sighed and then continued, "I expect that Bilshan's waiting outside to lead you around and fill you with stories about how important Capernaum was for Jesus. He and I tell competing stories. It's not about Galilee or Capernaum.

"I'm tired and getting a little wobbly. Thank you for coming." She stood up slowly, signaling for them to go. "If you will take the word of one who served Jesus from his first touch upon me, it's about Jesus."

Epiphany 6 / Ordinary Time 6
Mark 1:40-45
by Peter Andrew Smith

The Deserving Recipient

"Can you spare a quarter?" the disheveled man said with his hand outstretched.

Janine looked away and walked a little faster down the sidewalk. Sally stopped in front of him.

"Why do you need change?" she asked.

"I'm hungry. I haven't eaten in two days," he answered, running a hand through his unkempt beard.

She tilted her head to one side. "A quarter won't buy you much."

The man shrugged and wiped some dried mud off his tattered jacket. "If I ask for more, people don't give me anything."

"No one has stopped to help you yet today?" Sally asked, looking around at the people passing by them. Most had their eyes averted from the man. A few stared at him as they quickly walked past.

The man shook his head. "Not today. I'm awfully hungry. You have a quarter I could have?"

"Where do you live?" Sally asked.

"In the shelter most nights now. When it's warmer I sleep in the park."

"Sally," Janine said sharply from a distance down the sidewalk.

"I'll be right back," Sally said to the man.

"Sure," he replied. "You have a good day anyway, ma'am." He turned his back on her and went back to asking people for spare change.

"You shouldn't be talking to him," Janine whispered when Sally was close enough to hear. "That's crazy Steve Leroy."

"You know him?"

"Everyone knows about him in this town. He's a disappointment to his family and a blight on this community. He'll drink anything you give him."

"He said he is hungry," Sally said.

"Thirsty is more like it. Come on, I want to go to get a good seat at the movies." Janine took Sally's arm and started forward.

Sally shook herself free from Janine. "We've got lots of time. I've got to pick something up in the donut shop. I'll be back in a minute."

"Oh come on, Sally, we're going to be late," Janine protested, but Sally was already heading inside the nearby store.

Janine tapped her foot and stared at the sidewalk until Sally reappeared empty-handed.

"I thought you were getting something."

"I did," Sally said, walking past her to where Steve was still begging for change.

"Here," she said reaching into her pocket to pull something out. "This should get you something to eat."

"Thank you, ma'am," he said as he shook her hand. "God bless you, ma'am."

"God bless you too," Sally said as he headed off into the donut shop.

"You gave him money?" Janine said. "That was stupid. He's just going to spend it on booze or drugs."

Sally shook her head. "That was a gift card to the donut shop. He'll get himself a meal."

"Sally, you are such a sap. You can't help people like Steve Leroy. He had so much potential in his life and he wasted it. He doesn't deserve your kindness or your mercy."

"Everyone deserves kindness and mercy," Sally said.

Janine shook her head again. "You know what an attitude like that makes you?"

"Yes I do," Sally said. "A follower of Jesus."

Transfiguration of Our Lord
(Last Sunday after Epiphany)
Mark 9:2-9; Psalm 50:1-6
by Argile Smith

Listening

Raymond and Sylvia's marriage seemed to be over, or at least that's the impression that both of them shared after their last argument. For almost thirty years they had lived together as husband and wife, and at the beginning their relationship had been wonderful. They enjoyed each other's company, and they worked together to provide a loving home for their three children. But now they appeared to be arguing about everything.

In their fear that their marriage wouldn't survive another verbal outburst, they agreed that they needed to get some help, so they made an appointment to see their pastor. After one counseling session, their pastor referred them to Dr. Alexander, a well-qualified family counselor who had a long track record of success in helping couples get their marriage relationships back on track.

Sylvia made the appointment and together she and Raymond made their way to the counselor's office with more anxiety than either of them wanted to admit to one another. Dr. Alexander greeted them at the door and her warm smile and kindly ways calmed both of them. Almost immediately, their anxiety gave way to a sense of relief in the certainty that she would be able to help them get past their anger at one another. How they had prayed for someone to navigate them through the troubled waters of their marriage! They had no doubt that Dr. Alexander would serve as their compass and point them the way forward.

Not long into the session Dr. Alexander asked Raymond some questions about Sylvia, and she found his replies rather curious. For instance, she asked him to describe Sylvia's personal longings. Raymond replied with a litany of ways in which he had tried to help her to feel more confident. He went on and on about her insecurities and his constant efforts to help her overcome them. Then he proceeded to provide in rather tedious detail how her insecurities had emerged from her dysfunctional family relationships.

After a few minutes, Dr. Alexander interrupted Raymond by asking, "Raymond, would you repeat the question I asked you about Sylvia?"

"Of course," he replied, "I'll be happy to do it. You asked me to talk about Sylvia's insecurities, and I thought that you might appreciate some background information that would help you to understand why she seems to be having so much trouble with me and our marriage."

"Sylvia," Dr. Alexander asked, "what are Raymond's longings?"

"To be honest," she said, "Raymond longs to tell me what's wrong with me and how I should fix myself."

Raymond chimed in at that point to defend himself. "That's not altogether true, Dr. Alexander. I've known this woman longer than anyone else, and I think that I have some insight into her mind and heart and some, well, advice that'll help her to be a better person, a better mother, and a better wife."

"Raymond!" Dr. Alexander snapped. "You've shown me one problem in your marriage already. You, sir, don't know how to listen to your wife. You hear her say things, but you don't listen to what she's saying. I have a hunch that you don't listen to anybody else, either. I asked you to repeat the question I put to you about Sylvia's longings, but you didn't. Instead, you told me what you wanted me to know about her. You were not listening to me. You were only waiting for your turn to talk. When you got your turn, you didn't give anyone else a turn. I had to shout you down to get you to hush."

Although she may have hurt Raymond's feelings at first, in the long run she helped him. In a session a few weeks later, she explained to him that in snapping at him, she wanted to get his attention in a way that he would remember for a long time to come. For too long, she added, he had allowed himself to yammer on and on to Sylvia and to ignore what she was trying to say to him. Barking at him in the first session gave her the opportunity to teach him how much he needed to work on his listening skills.

Apparently Dr. Alexander's message to Raymond was loud and clear. He had gotten her point, and he had already begun to listen to Sylvia in a way that helped her. In turn, it helped their relationship. Dr. Alexander taught him how to listen to his wife with his eyes, his mind, his body, and his heart, as well as his ears.

God had to shout Peter down with the words "Listen to him!" Otherwise, Peter would have kept on talking and missing the point of Jesus' transfiguration (Mark 9:2-9). When "the Mighty One, God, the Lord has spoken," we do well to hush and listen (Psalm 50:1-6).

Ash Wednesday
Joel 2:1-2, 12-17
by C. David McKirachan

Sign of the Cross

Protestants don't do ashes. Yeah, I know. But it never made sense to me to deny people the gift of sensory blessing that anointing and ashes offer. Ashes are so clearly a mark of being part of something important — something important enough to wear on your forehead out in public. What? Are we so bent on fitting in, on being secular? Are we so focused on being non-Catholic that we can't claim our identity as Christians?

When I came to Shrewsbury, a nice, conservative, non-Catholic community, I suggested we offer ashes on Ash Wednesday and anointing on Maundy Thursday. I expected a minor hassle at least. But to my surprise, I had people thanking me.

George Bett was one of them. He had grown up in a Catholic neighborhood and felt left out on a few occasions. But on Ash Wednesday he felt something else. He thought it wasn't right that only Roman Catholics got to visibly demonstrate their Christianity and their acceptance of their mortality and their sin and their gratitude for the Savior's passion. After that sentence he had to take a breath. His wife Dorothy giggled. She does that a lot. She said, "Tell him what you did after you got the ashes, George." He hesitated. "Go on, tell David," she continued. "He has a right to know. It was his fault you demanded that we go grocery shopping after the 8:00 service. We had to find a grocery store that was open after 10:00 at night just so you could show off your ashes."

He looked down at her. She's diminutive. He smiled and replied, "Why should I tell him? You already did."

George was not a simple man. He was humble. He didn't believe in showing off. Well, maybe for his wife — he loved to hear her giggle. But he believed that first and foremost he was a Christian. And he was proud of it. Don't read "arrogant" there — I said "proud." His faith meant the world to him. He'd been through some places in his life when his faith was all he had. He wore those ashes as proudly as he wore his medals from the war. I never doubted that he knew that he'd done nothing to be proud of. He knew it was the mercy and the grace of God that had "left a blessing behind him."

I told that story at George's funeral, two days before Christmas the next year. I was tempted to open the casket before we buried him and make the sign of the cross on his forehead. He would have been proud.

Lent 1
Mark 1:9-15
by W. Lamar Massingill

Pain Is Generosity in Disguise

No human being can stonewall reality, not even Jesus as he traveled the earth as a human being. Regardless of how powerful we think we are, life is more powerful. It will take our pitiful attempts — our "stones," if you will — crush them, mix them with water, and have a drink.

After we learn that we cannot stop life's "stuff" from coming our way, we stand in our own wilderness — helpless, dripping wet, feeling heavy — and finally we begin asking the hopeful questions: What have I got going for me? How can I learn from this particular "stuff" that feels so bad? In the wilderness that Jesus was not led or directed into, but according to Mark driven into, Jesus spent forty days and forty nights learning what it meant to be Jesus. It was surely as painful, if not more so, than our own wildernesses. Perhaps even chaotic.

After thirty years of serving in ministry and as a hospice chaplain, and training as a therapist that I never really used, I have grown to learn, strange as it may sound to you who read this, that pain is generosity in disguise. I say that because it is precisely in the broken places that we grow up and on, and become not only stronger people but more compassionate (to suffer with) people who empathize with the wounds of others. In a word, we become what Henri Nouwen called "wounded healers."

During my tenure as a hospice chaplain, my patients taught me more about life than I taught them. Melvin, for example, taught me a most primal lesson. In fact, it was the beginning of what I would grow to believe and do still — namely, that chaos is the very raw material out of which we experience grace.

While I was Melvin's spiritual caregiver years ago, I asked him what was the one thing that had most enriched his life. To my surprise he answered, "Being diagnosed with cancer. It has opened my eyes to what really matters in life as nothing else has ever done. The practice of unwrapping everything, even the chaotic, with the hands of gratitude is the way to unending discoveries of God's gifts."

Incredible. If we trust that grace is enough to care for us, then that trust keeps us reconciled and committed to live with whatever life soaks us with. The Holy One is constantly taking our own chaos and pain, as he did the chaos of Jesus in the wilderness, and like a generous alchemist turning it into something mysteriously miraculous and meant to teach us. Are there reasons not to trust this? I think not. I think not.

Lent 2
Mark 8:31-38; Psalm 22:23-31
by Frank Ramirez

Donkey Cross

The cross is the central symbol of our faith. We can be very casual about wearing the cross around the neck or on the lapel. We sometimes forget, however, that the cross is a symbol of terror, despair, horror, degradation, agony, and humiliation. It was a form of execution reserved for the lowest of the low, for those outside the pale of humanity, whose bodies would be dumped in the garbage heaps afterward to be torn apart by wild dogs. Indeed, whenever a portion of the New Testament was read aloud, first-century listeners must have cringed every time they heard the word "cross." It was that obscene.

So shameful was the image of the cross to our ancestors in the faith, so obscene the method of execution, that for over four centuries the church chose not to use that symbol in its art.

Well, there is one example of the cross used in a drawing from early Christian history, but it was drawn by an opponent of the faith. This piece of graffiti in the slave quarters of the Imperial Palace in Rome shows a crude drawing of a crucifixion. On the cross hung a man with the head of a donkey. At the feet of the victim is an individual engaged in adoration. There's a single line written beneath it: "Alexamenos worships his god."

This anti-Christian drawing makes it clear how shameful the cross could be. Even so, this Alexamenos was not ashamed to claim Jesus as Lord, even though it led to ridicule. It helps us realize why Christians did not wear the cross as a symbol for over four centuries.

More important than whether we wear the cross is whether we bear the cross. Anna Mow was a missionary, mother, writer, and teacher, an active speaker and much-loved disciple of Jesus Christ. She seemed willing to endure anything for the sake of her Savior. Perhaps that's why it seemed so ironic that one who was such a great communicator should suffer a debilitating stroke late in life that made it nearly impossible for her to communicate.

Despite a stroke that limited her ability to write and speak, she dictated a final book to demonstrate her determination to bear the cross. Anna's book is sparkling bright as a running brook in spring, yet filled with the same brooding depth of a pond deep from the melting snows. In a helpless condition she describes as "a world of suffering," Anna writes, "I can't even choose what kind of suffering I'll have. But I can choose what my attitude is going to be toward suffering."

Calling upon the example of Job, Anna differentiates between a God who sends suffering and one who permits it. "No matter what happens to us, we are within his loving care. Our Lord suffered. Paul's thorn in the flesh was never taken away. We may suffer. If we trust him, the suffering will never be useless."

And then there's this: "No one is ever useless to God. No one who can pray is ever useless. There are many people to perform the needed activities, but too few to take the time for prayer." (From *Two or Ninety-Two* by Anna Mow [Brethren Press].)

The cross as an instrument of torture also represents the intersection of two roads. It is the place where heaven and earth come together. It is the spot where we meet Jesus.

Lent 3
Exodus 20:1-17
by C. David McKirachan

Traffic Control

My father always talked about the Ten Commandments as God's green lights. He saw them as rules by which we can get along better. It kind of flew in the face of the "thou shall not..." mentality with which we often approach the Decalogue.

In seminary I was given another angle on this cornerstone of our covenant. My professor spoke of a community of escaped slaves who needed something other than rules that enforced a top-down authority — they had just escaped from such authority. God was not about to give them something that put them back into another oppressive system.

Armed with these insights I went into my first pastorate, a small church on the border of inner-city Newark, New Jersey. I had more energy than sense. We had no money for curriculum, nobody who had any opportunity or experience teaching. So I wrote a lesson plan and prepared to be the teacher, the only teacher for a two-week Vacation Bible School.

Sixteen kids between the ages of six and fifteen years signed up. The plan was simple; survive and keep them engaged. This demanded a lot of hands-on group activity. So what better way to engage a bunch of kids than to build a few pyramids and make a few bricks? I turned them into slaves under the lash of Pharaoh's rule. Naturally, I was the king/god of the Upper and Lower Nile. We did exercises with work and family dynamics and food and random authority.

All week long they did and undid things at my whim. They got snacks or none because I said so. Along the way we did crafts, sang songs, prayed, read the Bible (a lot from Genesis and Exodus), and played games.

They all came back for the second week. I was amazed.

We went through the story of Moses and the exodus — plagues and all. (They really liked the frogs.) The passage through the sea and the destruction of Pharaoh's army was fun to act out — they had to bring extra clothes that day. (The water fight went on for quite a while.) Finally we made it to the mountain of revelation, the mountain of the Law. Moses went up the mountain into the cloud. I asked them what rules, what guidelines for getting along in their new freedom, they thought God would give them.

After much hassle and discussion they came up with five rules. These kids blew me away:

Nobody's God but God.
You get to keep what belongs to you.
Nobody gets to kill anybody else.
Families can't be broken up.
Everybody gets a day off.

Aside from the clear harmony between our Decalogue and the kids' pentalogue, it became very clear to me that the commandments that were given to us on that mountaintop were not arbitrary or esoteric but were totally linked to the experience of the community to whom they were given. God's inspiration can be seen in the harmony these simple rules create for all who seek to live them out in the promise of freedom and hope — whether they are escaping from Pharaoh's yoke or are seeking to live in community in the land of milk and honey.

The pizza guy down at the corner gave us six pies for our final party. He told me he was grateful to me for keeping the little monsters off the street. So much for enlightenment....

Lent 4
Numbers 21:4-9
by Larry Winebrenner

Sympathetic Magic

Anthropologists who read Numbers 21:4-9 often refer to the passage as practicing sympathetic magic, which is causing an effect by using an item similar to the situation at hand. Thus, poisonous serpents cause a problem; bronze serpents cure the problem. The anthropologists who take this position believe Moses learned about sympathetic magic while growing up in Pharaoh's household.

Of course, there may have been reasons that sympathetic magic was intended here. If the community came out of a culture where sympathetic magic was the norm it might be better understood than other approaches. Also, even if sympathetic magic was not the purpose of the bronze serpent, still, the physical figure of the snake kept before the people both that they had been rebellious and that the power of God was at work.

For those of us raised in the rational-scientific materialism worldview, there is another message. We can never second-guess what God will or will not do. Neither will we ever be able to dictate the ways in which God's wonders may be performed.

Sympathetic magic? Immediate miracle? Natural explanation? It matters not. God's wonders the Lord will perform.

Lent 5
John 12:20-33
by Peter Andrew Smith

Showing Them Jesus

"Show me Jesus," the young man said to the pastor. "Someone told me that you talk about his life and miracles on Sunday. Show me this Messiah who came to save the world."

The pastor took the young man into the church hall. The hall was filled with tables, chairs, and the smell of hot food. There was a line of people waiting.

"Help serve this meal," the pastor said to the young man.

The young man was confused but made his way to the kitchen. An elderly woman motioned him inside and handed him a potato and a small knife. They worked in silence peeling a large bag of potatoes. When the bag was empty the young man looked around.

"I'm not sure what to do," he said.

"Why did you come here today?" the elderly woman asked.

"I want to see Jesus," the young man replied.

"Then why don't you go up front and help dish out the food?"

The young man moved up front and took a place in the line spooning soup into bowls for people as they passed by. An old man smiled and thanked the young man as he grasped his bowl of soup.

"Why are you thanking me?" he asked the old man.

"Because I am cold and hungry and this is a hot meal."

"But all I did was peel potatoes," the young man said. "I didn't even come here to serve a meal today."

"Then why did you come here?"

"I came here because I want to find Jesus," the young man said.

"He is certainly in this place. God bless you for helping me."

The young man blushed and went back to giving food to the other people in line. He was surprised because he expected them to be old and dirty. Yet people old and young passed before him. Some had grubby clothes, while others were freshly scrubbed. There were people by themselves, and others who brought their families. As he handed a bowl to a young woman, he realized that he knew her from school.

"Hi," he said awkwardly.

She smiled and thanked him like everyone else. He turned to give soup to the next person when a man put a bowl into his hands.

"You've been working hard. Have something to eat," the man said.

"But I didn't come here to eat."

"Why did you come here?" the man asked.

"I came here to know Jesus."

"Then go and sit with the people he loves," the man said, gesturing at the crowd eating at the tables before turning back to serve the next person soup.

The young man took his bowl and started forward toward the tables, unsure and uncertain. The young woman who knew him from school pointed at a seat next to her.

"Come sit with me," she said. "There is always room for another person here."

The young man sat and ate his soup quietly. He expected everyone to just sit in silence and eat. Yet he found himself surrounded by the buzz of conversation punctuated with laughter, and even in one corner some singing. As the young man sipped at his soup he listened as the people talked and chatted with each other. Soon others joined them at the table and he found himself being drawn into the conversation and laughter.

"Everyone seems so happy," he said.

"The soup is hot and the day is cold," the young woman said. "This is a good place if you are hungry and lost. I've not seen you here before; what brings you here today?"

"I asked the pastor to show me Jesus," the young man said.

"And have you seen him?"

"I've seen people working together to help other people and I've seen hungry people fed," the young man said. "But I'm not sure I've seen Jesus."

"Maybe you need to know why the people are doing those things," the young woman said.

"Why are you here?" he asked.

"Because I was hungry and I know that when I come here I am fed with more than just food," she said as she took her empty bowl to the kitchen to be washed.

The young man went to the man serving soup to those waiting in line. "Why do you give food to these people?"

"Jesus asks me to feed the hungry," the man said.

The young man went into the kitchen and asked, "Why do you prepare the food for people you do not know?"

"Because Jesus tells me to love my neighbor," the elderly woman replied.

The young man went back to the hall and saw the pastor eating soup at a table. He sat next to him.

"I asked you to show me Jesus," the young man said.

"Did you see him?" the pastor asked. "Did you see his love and concern for others, the generosity of his heart, and the change he brings into people's lives?"

The young man thought for a moment and nodded. "I think I'll come back and help tomorrow, and come to church on Sunday too."

The pastor smiled. "Then you have done something more than simply see Jesus. You have begun to follow him."

Passion / Palm Sunday
Mark 14:1—15:47
by C. David McKirachan

Holiday for Losers

Bible studies are the bread and butter of my ministry. I love to preach and people tell me that's why they come to church — because they never know what's going to happen in that part of the service titled "Sermon." But teaching the Bible and spiritual formation is the place where people get to share and care and become linked with each other as the active and bonding Body of Christ. I consider Bible studies to be the engine that drives the church.

All that goes to say that I'm deeply invested in the process of teaching, which includes equal amounts of listening and informing and flying kites to attract any kind of lightning available. But I'm telling you, I didn't expect this one.

We were doing a Lenten study on Christ's journey to the cross. I tend to pick up on lightweight subjects like that during Lent: evil, suffering, spiritual disciplines… subjects that make people wonder why they came to this stupid class in the first place. We have the meetings in my home — it invites informality. (I also know where the exits are.) This particular study's goal was to help the students visualize, hear, smell, feel, and walk with the Lord as he went from triumph to tomb. It got graphic and confrontive and theological all at the same time. In other words, it was working.

We got down to the Lord's role in the whole thing. We talked about victims, heroes, political showmen, self-flagellating religious freaks, and every other available heretical and orthodox role I or they could come up with. The Passion doesn't let us off easy here. He's too real to fit any convenient category.

One member of the class was a fairly successful entrepreneur in his early sixties who was very much in control of his life and liked to be significant wherever he went. He needed managing in class because he tended to hold forth if given the chance. On this evening he'd gotten quiet. I should have felt the barometer falling. There was a storm building and it suddenly burst forth from him, loudly. "This is nuts. Why do you insist on pushing this idea that Jesus was a wimp? If he acted like you say he did, he was a loser. It's like this forgiveness thing. It makes no sense. You're all a bunch of wimps...."

Those dots are a minimalist way of saying that he went on from there. Managing a class is one thing. Handling an outburst from somebody who is used to treating every circumstance competitively and winning all competitions is another.

I wanted to dismiss him. I would have loved to throw him out of the class. However, when a kite attracts lightning it's time to consider the source. I let him wind down a little and said, "You know, I think you're right." I thought he'd popped a vessel. His eyes almost fell out of his head. He said, "I am?" The room erupted. It was one of those moments that teachers live for. The discussion that followed cut through all the nice words and platitudes that pad and neaten the cross. A few people cried. One person kept saying, "Why would he do that for me?"

I really feel like the Lord stood there with us that evening. It wasn't easy or pretty or convenient or fun. But it was meaningful and powerful and cut right to the bone of our sin that refuses to see him clearly.

I wish I could say Mr. Winner changed. He's still trapped. But it taught this teacher something. It taught me to let the Lord stand up for himself. It let me see him again. It let me marvel again. It convicted me. The cross will do that, if you let it. It just stands there above all the "... wreaks of time."

All we have to do is gather there at its foot. I do that every year, with all the rest of the losers. I can't think of a place I'd rather be.

Maundy Thursday
John 13:1-17, 31b-35
by David O. Bales

One More Passover

    Peter roused slowly from sleep and tried to roll from his side to his back but the chains stopped him. The dampness of the rocks beneath him gave him a shiver that woke him more. He told himself to open his eyes but even though the dark promised no extra pain for his eyes, he was so exhausted that after one glimpse of the dim gloom surrounding him and his fellow prisoners, he settled again onto his left side. He shifted, slid his hip slightly to try to move off a sharp stone, then gave up and stayed where he was.
    Almost no energy left, he thought. He had the will. Peter always had the will, but now, nearly starved in Rome's prison and surely awaiting execution, he no longer had the wherewithal. Not even a good place to lay his head, just as Jesus had said about himself. In these last few days, as he was beaten and interrogated, he more and more thought of Jesus — what he'd done and said and what Peter now understood better about him.
    Not much else to do there in the dark but think. A younger man near him whimpered a lot. An older man was brought in last night. He couldn't see him well, but he was limp and bleeding and he felt his sticky blood beside him and he no longer heard his breathing. All signs that he was dead, just as Jesus was dead on the cross. Romans killed him. Romans were good at death. When they dragged this man from beside him, they'd guarantee his death by pushing a sword into his stomach, just as they thrust a javelin into Jesus' side.
    Peter had known he couldn't continue in Rome much longer. He'd heard reports of the rumors going around about

the strange Jews and their stranger cousins, the Christians. People told him what was being said, repeated, and exaggerated. Some told him as a warning, others enjoyed trying to frighten this odd, aged preacher. He and his students discussed leaving Rome but Peter wanted to stay for Passover in order to share that special night with his students and Rome's few but endangered believers.

He sighed, then realized he had awakened himself snoring. While slightly awake again his mind returned to his last thought before sleeping. He had wanted to share the Passover one more time. Every time he'd celebrated Passover in these last thirty years he felt not only that the risen Jesus was closer to him, Peter also came to understand more of what the earthly Jesus meant.

"Lord, are you going to wash my feet?" He'd been horrified: Israel's Messiah stooping down as the lowest slave washing his feet. Not that Peter minded Jesus doing things for him. Peter expected Jesus to do things for him, but he expected to receive them after Jesus sat on the throne of the free nation of Israel. Peter expected great favors. For instance, he'd been willing to accept all the royal plantations along the eastern shore of the great sea, or even to continue to serve in Jesus' administration, perhaps helping to maintain peace within the neighboring nations after Jesus' armies defeated them.

Peter wasn't any more dense than the rest of Jesus' students. Peter realized that and was now able, finally, to forgive himself, although Jesus had forgiven him decades before. However, Peter had needed time to thoroughly grasp what Jesus meant and that understanding continued to grow when the risen Jesus healed people through Peter's hands. It grew when Peter watched ordinary people come to faith and then live with extraordinary hope and love. Peter's understanding of Jesus grew with his own travels and troubles and with his own students' openness and obtuseness.

Jesus had told Peter that he'd understand later but even then Peter said, "You will never wash my feet." Again Peter's consciousness fluttered between sleep and waking. His understanding had expanded toward eternal dimensions at Jesus' resurrection. What a flash from heaven to earth! What godly thunder rattling the brains of humanity! Jesus was alive again, eating with them, teaching them, granting them the forgiveness they were authorized joyfully to give to others. Such was Peter's central message: Jesus' resurrection. He grew more and more to understand Jesus, even as the Jewish and Gentile Christians disagreed and people like Paul proclaimed Jesus from a different perspective. And... even when Peter's wife died.

The old man Peter, shackled in the wet, dark Roman detention, had wanted once more to share Passover. Jesus, bowing at Peter's feet, had said, "Unless I wash you, you have no share in me."

If only one more time... the Passover, Lord.

He heard a low voice from outside. Now louder and feet echoing. Two soldiers, maybe three. Four soldiers. The death squad approached the door and the giant key turned in the lock. The door squeaked... more light. A prisoner across the room began to cry for his mother. They came only for Peter. They grabbed him roughly and began to unshackle him. Peter spoke the phrase he'd learned to repeat when he didn't exactly understand Jesus or didn't know precisely what to do. "Lord, not my feet only but also my hands and head."

Good Friday
Isaiah 52:13—53:12
by Peter Andrew Smith

Healed by His Wounds

"Quite honestly, Pastor, I'm not doing that well," John said as he let go of his pastor's hand and lay back in the bed. "It feels like the chemotherapy is still tearing out my insides."

"The last round was a few days ago, wasn't it?" Pastor Tim said, looking at the flow of medicine moving through the intravenous drip which ran into John's arm. "Is that for the pain?"

"Yeah. The doctor said it should pass and I'll feel better tomorrow or the next day."

A smile crossed Pastor Tim's face. "Well then, maybe the weekend will look brighter."

"I don't think so," John said. "It was all for nothing."

"Oh?"

"Yeah, I got the test results back and the tumor has spread. The doctor said they could try another round of chemotherapy, but I refused. I don't want to spend the days I have left feeling sick because of drugs."

"The cancer is that progressed?"

"It is. They all say there is really nothing they can do but keep me comfortable."

Pastor Tim's eyes watered up. "I'm so sorry, John. We all have been praying and hoping for a better result from the tests."

John took his pastor's hand again. "I know. You and all the church have been so good to me. Being so far away from the kids makes this so much harder."

"Are they coming?"

"They're flying in tomorrow. Julie is coming with the baby." John closed his eyes and grimaced.

"Do you want me to get the nurse?"

John shook his head. "What they are giving me is keeping the pain down."

"Is there anything I can do?"

John looked his pastor in the eyes. "Tell me why."

"Pardon?"

"Why is this happening to me? I've tried to live a good life and be a faithful Christian. I provided for my family and never cheated on Laura all the years we were married. I wasn't perfect but I was a good man. Why is my life going to end like this?"

"I honestly don't know why this is happening, John."

"I feel so torn apart inside, and I'm not talking about the side effects from the drugs. I'm so angry with God right now and...." John threw his hands up and slumped back in the bed. "How can he know what I'm going through? How can God possibly understand my pain sitting up in heaven?"

"Can I read you something?"

John shrugged and closed his eyes once more.

Pastor Tim began to read from Isaiah. "See, my servant shall prosper...."

John didn't move as the passage was read, but his eyes snapped open with the words "He was despised and rejected by others; a man of suffering and acquainted with infirmity...."

Pastor Tim finished the passage and started to close the book.

"Let me see," John said, and he took the opened Bible and laid it on his lap. His fingers traced the words and his lips moved slightly as he read. When he reached the end of the passage tears were streaming down his face. "I never knew. I've heard those words before, but I never knew."

"Knew what, John?"

"That God really does understand. Jesus suffered. He really suffered, and through that suffering comes Easter," John replied. "I tried to be upbeat in my prayers, even when my life was falling apart. I was afraid to show God my weakness and confusion. I didn't think he could understand and thought somehow I wasn't worthy of Jesus because I was suffering."

"God loves you no matter what is happening in your life," Pastor Tim said. "The promise of the resurrection is not for the healthy but for the sick."

"I knew that up here," John said, touching his forehead and then resting his hand on his chest. "But now I know it in here. Pastor, can we pray?"

"Of course, John." Pastor Tim bowed his head and opened his mouth, but before he could say anything John began to speak.

"Jesus, you understand my pain and my fear...."

Easter Day
John 20:1-18
by W. Lamar Massingill

There Is No Death, Just Life

You have to admit that in some sense we feel like death is annihilation, a cement floor waiting for a falling light bulb. But what if what Gail Sheehy once called "the dark at the end of the tunnel" (her metaphor for death) could somehow lose its foreboding control over us and turn into "the light at the end of the tunnel" instead?

I remember a play written years ago by Eugene O'Neill, one of America's great playwrights, called *Lazarus Laughed*. It was by no means a commercial success but I think its depth of wisdom would serve to inform us about our fear of death. Reading the work proved to be a profound spiritual experience for me, to the extent that I recognized the freedom that would happen if we did not fear death as much as we do.

O'Neill picks up where the biblical story about Lazarus leaves off. That is, at the beginning of the play Jesus has just called Lazarus back from three days in the tomb and has instructed that he be unbound. O'Neill has Lazarus coming out of the tomb laughing — not a bitter, scornful laugh, but a gentle, tender kind of sound. He doesn't have a faraway look in his eyes but rather seems to see the people closest to him with a new kind of delight and affection. He embraces his sisters Mary and Martha. He embraces the friend who brought about this miracle. He pats the earth with wonder. He looks up to the sky with an astonishing sense of delight. It is as if everything has taken on a new luster because of what he has learned.

After Lazarus has gone home and all the excitement of his return has begun to settle, people inevitably begin to ask

Lazarus the primal question on all their minds: "Lazarus, what is it like to die? What is it like to move into that portal, that entrance into what is unknown?"

Lazarus begins to laugh that gentle, wonderful laughter of delight, and he opens his mouth and says, "There is only life; there is only God; there is nothing to fear. Death is not what it looks like from this side. It is not an abyss into which we fall; it is an exit through which we move. It simply opens into greater light, into a realm of everlasting change. There is nothing out there to fear, for there is only life; there is only God. Therefore we don't have to be afraid anymore. The object of life is not to avoid death but to learn to live. We must learn to embrace the earth the way God embraces it, to love each other, to affirm each other, to help the whole creation grow. Do not be afraid," Lazarus keeps saying, "there is nothing to fear, there is only life."

As the play unfolds, Lazarus embodies what it would mean to be freed of death. His house becomes the house of laughter. There is music and dancing there day and night, and as he continues to live in this free and wonderful way, other human beings are caught up in the joyfulness of it. They cease to be afraid. They start being generous and humane with one another. They fall back into the delight of life itself. They participate in God's delight over creation. And these realities begin to spread throughout the entire community.

The Roman officials notice this and they, like most controlling people, become disturbed at all this laughing. Remember, there is nothing more dangerous to a tyrant than a person who has lost his fear of death. How do you intimidate such a person? How do you grind him into obedience? So Lazarus is finally arrested by the Roman authorities, and they say, "Lazarus, you have to stop this incessant laughter. You do it now, or we will punish you." And Lazarus continues to laugh and say, "There is no death, there is only life."

And not being able to stop Lazarus, they finally ship him to Rome where he is ushered into the presence of the emperor himself. In frustration, the emperor says the same thing: "Stop it, Lazarus. Stop this laughter. If you do not stop, I'm going to have you killed."

Which was answered only by a continuous kind of laughter, with Lazarus saying, "Go ahead. You have no power over me ultimately. There is no death, there is only life." The play ends with the laughing Lazarus having conquered the emperor of Rome because his fear of death has been conquered forever.

Here I think that O'Neill has put his finger on the functional power of what would happen if the dark at the end of the tunnel ever lost its control over human beings.

Remember: There is no death, there is only life. There is only God.

Easter 2
John 20:19-31
by Keith Hewitt

Doubt

If you believe nothing else of what I tell you, believe this: I never doubted.

I never doubted the Master. During the time I traveled with him, the time I lived with him and learned from him, I felt many things: confusion, hope, love, fear, even an occasional glimmer of understanding — you name it and I probably experienced it some time during those three years. But I can honestly say I never doubted him. If you think I did, then you're buying into the spin.

To understand where I'm coming from, you have to understand what those last days were like. For months beforehand, Jesus had been telling us that the end — his end — was near. First indirectly, and then more and more directly as time went on, he told us that he would soon die. We put on a bold face for the world, but we fretted over that, talked about it among ourselves, tried to understand why he would say such a thing. We didn't understand how he could be so sure that he would be treated that way.

Then that Sunday, that glorious day, all those worries were swept away as we entered Jerusalem like peaceful conquerors — he rode in to cheering crowds waving palm fronds, total strangers throwing their cloaks on the ground for his donkey to walk upon. We rode the crest of that incredible wave, with a man that we convinced ourselves we had misunderstood, that this was not a man on a path to destruction but a prophet on a path to glory.

And then… and then…

Then came the arrest at our place of refuge, when we scattered like frightened birds, hardly looking back to see what had happened, only to see if the guards were on our trail too. That was followed by the night of terror for us, fear that the authorities would not content themselves with the root of the rebellion but might come after the fragile shoots that it had nourished. Scattered, running when no one pursued, hiding with friends or in dark alleys — always with an ear cocked to the night, waiting for the pounding on the door or the shout in the dark that would tell us our time had come too.

There was the trial (if you call it that), where none of us came forward to defend him or even dared to show our face to the authorities. The one man who came closest to him that night, who almost stood with the Master in the face of overwhelming power, still denied knowing him when someone picked him out of the crowd and fled back into the darkness to nurse the knot of shame that burned in his belly. He found me that night and told me what he had done, though I could barely understand him through the sobs — and then I held him for the night, cradling his head as he wept like a child, wept for the ordeal our Master would face, wept for knowing how he had broken and run.

Only one of us dared to stand by the cross the next day while Jesus poured out his life upon the rocky soil of Golgotha. Even so, it was not one of us who stepped forward that afternoon to claim the body, who dared to ask permission to take him down from that damned thing and give him a proper burial, rather than be left hanging for the crows and the dogs or pulled down and thrown into the Valley of Gehenna with the trash.

We did not dare ask such a "favor," but hid and plumbed the depths of our own hells while this near-stranger stepped forward. We hid while the old man and the women took Jesus down and did him one last kindness. I would like to say that it wasn't so, but it was. We — his disciples — stood by and did nothing. Not even a week had gone by since we entered Jerusalem feeling like princes-to-be... and there we were, like rats in the dark.

Saturday was another day of torment, another day of questions, another day of waiting for our own personal worlds to end. By nightfall, we began to believe that maybe we would not be rounded up. We started to gather, in twos and threes, to tell each other about our own narrow escapes, to describe how close we came to the Master's fate, all the while knowing that every word was bluster, finally collapsing into shared misery, equal parts grief and self-pity.

That night, too, passed slowly. I was not with the group that the women sought out the next morning — I was not there when they set hearts racing by suddenly pounding on the door before the light had penetrated to the deepest corners of Jerusalem, making all inside believe that their time had come after all. I was not there when the women babbled of an empty tomb, or when several of the disciples raced to that tomb to see for themselves what the women had seen... or not seen. I was not there but I can imagine what a picture it must have been.

I can imagine the confusion, the panic, and the disbelief that gripped them.

I wasn't there that night, in the safe house where most of my companions had gathered to discuss what had happened, to try to figure out where the Master's body had gone, because even then — even with the women reporting that they had seen him themselves — it was just not to be believed. Women, after all, were prone to hysteria and under the circumstances they might believe they had seen anything. Leave it to the men to figure out: the men who had deserted him and hid themselves for three days.

They were still pondering this mystery when he appeared among them. I know that because they told me... they told me how one moment they were arguing among themselves and the next he was there, standing among them. Instead of fear, even instead of shock, calm rippled out from his presence. He spoke to them and they finally understood; he spoke to them and their fears drained away; he spoke to them and they knew that everything had happened according to plan.

They spoke to me and I wasn't ready to believe. They talked to me for days, told me how foolish I was, told me how wrong I was, but I did not believe. It wasn't until I stood in the room with them a week later and saw his glorious face — when I saw those hands and the scars on his body — that I believed.

But you see, it's not that I didn't believe in the Master. When I look back now, I can understand quite a bit of what he had told us, understand that he was trying to prepare us to think about the unthinkable, endure the unendurable. He was telling us about a grand plan, when all we wanted to know was "What about us?"

When I looked back on the days of his arrest, trial, and execution... the days we separated ourselves from him in fear rather than reaching out for him in love, I wondered. How could he have done so much, and we so little, and he would still come back to people like us?

I never doubted the Master, I just didn't understand why he would come back to us. It wasn't until that night, when I finally did look upon his face, when I saw the love in his eyes, when he reached out to me like an old friend back from a long journey that I understood.

I understood that it needed no understanding... that's what grace is all about.

And I wept once more.

Easter 3
Luke 24:36b-48
by David O. Bales

The Whole Truth

Luke was no slouch as a writer. He could compose long, convoluted Greek sentences that took half a page to complete. Then, dipping the stylus again into the ink, he could suddenly make words on papyrus sound like a stiff 300-year-old translation of Hebrew into Greek. He would subtly repeat themes and patterns of God's grace to help readers hear the Hebrew Old Testament echo in Jesus' life and teaching. The man was a master at clarity: never a word out of place, nor could anyone misunderstand his intent. If one only read his final draft, Luke seemed to be in full command of his subject.

His subject, however, was Jesus, and Jesus had been raised from the dead. No editing job as Luke rewrote Mark's gospel would or should undo the central fact of Jesus' resurrection. Within a few decades the faith had grown out of Judea, and the new religion of Jesus was spreading through the eastern Mediterranean world — even showing up in the city of Rome. This faith depended upon the truth of Jesus' resurrection.

Luke sat at his writing table. A good writer, yes; a careful historian, of course; a believer in the risen Jesus, always. But in his reporting of Jesus' resurrection appearances, he'd gotten jittery. Luke had his sources. He'd heard the stories passed on from the first eyewitnesses. Jesus' resurrection was the tip of God's new world invading human existence. But as an architect doubts his abilities when asked to design the most imposing structure in the world, so Luke the writer fumbled for words to describe Jesus' three resurrection appearances.

Halfway through recording Jesus' resurrection appearances, Luke had gasped, slammed his hands on the writing table, and stopped his writing. He'd let his manuscript sit for weeks. Years of work just laid upon a shelf. Daily he walked by the scroll and then quickly left the room. He had a few fingers' width of space remaining blank on the bottom of the papyrus for the writing of what seemed incredible.

Decades before, Paul the apostle had also stumbled around trying to describe the resurrection. He'd attempted to do so by talking about different kinds of bodies and the way seeds change after sprouting. Paul had struggled to explain what Luke now must portray in order to finish his gospel.

Jesus had been alive and free of the tomb, talking to his students, and even eating with them. Luke was sure of this. He'd interviewed many of the first Christians. They'd told him about Jesus simply showing up in their midst. However, if they'd thought Jesus was a ghost, how could Luke, merely by writing, convince people otherwise? If Jesus' disciples assumed the resurrection was too good to be true, could Luke reduce it to papyrus and make it seem anything but untrue?

Talk about writer's block! He prayed, and he checked his notes and written sources again. He discussed the problem with his fellow Christians, and he waited — almost like Jesus told his students to wait in Jerusalem for the power from on high.

Then early one Sunday morning, he had it. During a worship gathering a preacher had talked about Jesus' resurrection. Luke had watched Jesus' resurrection appearances in his mind as he heard them. Like a waking dream, he'd taken part in the disciples' experience of Jesus being alive again. By an answer to prayer or profound insight, whatever anyone wanted to name it, Luke realized that he needed to tell the whole truth. In obedience to God he should record the entire story — not just that Jesus came out of nowhere while the disciples talked, not just that he commanded them to touch him and reassured them that ghosts weren't made of flesh and blood, not just that he showed them his hands and feet, not just that he ate their broiled fish. Luke realized that, in order for readers to truly accept Jesus' final appearance to his disciples, he needed to record all the truth. Jesus' resurrection wasn't just about Jesus, but also about the people he appeared to. Luke must tell as much about what Jesus' friends experienced as about what Jesus said and did. He dashed into the room where his document about Jesus waited on the shelf.

Luke pulled out the notes about Jesus after his resurrection. He began to copy the events but he would halt in his copying to include what he'd been told about Jesus' students. "They were startled and terrified, and thought they were seeing a ghost." He continued reporting Jesus' appearance but he added that doubts arose in their hearts. He told of how Jesus dealt matter-of-factly with their amazement. Luke then inserted "in their joy they were disbelieving and still wondering." There it was — the whole truth. He continued the last sentences to describe Jesus' ascension. He pushed the scroll to the side, put his face in his hands, and wept. The whole truth about Jesus' resurrection was now written, and it was almost — but not quite — too good to be true.

Easter 4
John 10:11-18; Psalm 23
by Frank Ramirez

The Goat Shepherd

The little town of Everett, Pennsylvania, partway between Philadelphia and Pittsburgh, used to lie right on US 30, the old Lincoln Highway that runs all the way across the United States. Then the town was bypassed, which certainly sped up traffic for those rushing on the east-west highway but also helped motorists drive past the little town without stopping for something to eat. This small town shares the same difficulties that folks have across the country — lack of jobs, for instance, drug use, and education. But people still love the town and love to live there.

Main Street is two miles long. As you leave the town going east you climb a little hill and then merge with the Lincoln Highway. There are steep cliffs rising to your right as you wind under the main road before joining it. Large trucks barrel down off the bypass so you have to be a little careful. One of the biggest problems is that there is a distraction — there are flocks of wild goats that feed on those steep hills. Adult goats and little kids hop easily from stone to stone on the steep cliffs. These are graceful animals who seem to have little trouble surviving in what would be a hostile environment for most people.

According to local legend, a farmer bought them to keep down the weeds but they refused to cooperate. They ate what they wanted, not what he wanted. He is said to have driven them away when he grew tired of paying for feed. The flocks thrived.

So the problem is not the goats but the drivers who spot them and crane their necks to see how they're doing. Folks know they're out there. They might be missing for a month or a season. Perhaps they have migrated to better feeding grounds. But eventually they return — and when they come back people want to see them. Then people start talking about them. Folks at the diner will not only talk about seeing goats but which ones. They have nicknames for the goats, depending on their appearance. And they are happy to see old friends return on those hillsides.

The authorities have tried to remove the goats on occasion because they want to prevent possible accidents by the rubberneckers — with little success. But things came to a head a year ago when a couple of goats, well known around the town, experienced a new difficulty. One of them broke a leg and disappeared, then the other one disappeared. Letters to the editor of the local newspaper demanded an investigation. Prosecutions were demanded. Finally letters from animal organizations appeared to assure folks that the injured goat was being cared for in a secure but hidden location and that once healthy it would be returned into the wild.

Some might wonder why it is that with problems that seem too great to handle a town would worry about a couple of goats. But folks know these goats. The goats are individuals to them. And that's the perspective of the shepherd toward the flock, whether it's a flock of goats or, as in the case of this week's Bible passages, a flock of sheep. The Good Shepherd knows every member of the flock. They are all individuals. They are missed when they are gone. The Good Shepherd will never discount any member of the flock and will search for anyone that is lost — and will even lay down a life to protect the flock.

And that's how we look to God. There are no disposable members of the human family. If we are lost members of the flock, Jesus will look for us. Because we were in danger of eternal death because of our sins, Jesus was willing to die for us. God knows us all by name. We are personalities to the creator. We are talked about around the coffee pot in heaven. That's a comforting thought.

Easter 5
John 15:1-8
by C. David McKirachan

Family Resemblance

I worked in Lake Placid, Florida, two summers during college. My brother was director of the Presbyterian Conference Center in Lake Placid, which is a few miles from Sebring, out by Okeechobee. It's farm country. They call it muck farming. It's proto-peat, all organic and shimmies like jello. It doesn't smell too sweet and the decomposing material that produces the smell acts like compost. Stuff grows out there like it's trying to get away from the stinky jello.

When we were first driving into the area, we passed some fields that looked like they'd come from a science fiction movie. Tree stumps about four or five feet tall, cut off and painted white, went on as far as the eye could see. It was weird. It took me all of thirty seconds to ask my brother, "What the heck happened there?"

He explained that it was a citrus grove. They grow lemon trees, being the hardiest of the breed, and when they get to a certain height they chop them off, paint them white, let them sit for a little while, and then graft whatever fruit they want onto the lemon stumps. So grapefruits, oranges, tangerines, and more are all grown on lemon stumps. I don't know if he was spouting (he had the same blarney blood in his veins as I do), but the whole thing sounded interesting. All those fruits depended on the lowly lemon for their propagation and their health.

Being grafted to the vine of the Lord is basic for us if we are to flourish. Not because we'll get fried by an angry God but because it makes sense. If we are to bear the fruit of life, if our lives are to be something more than scrambles toward the grave, we need to be grafted to the one who demonstrates the nature of eternity in the flesh.

The other interesting part of this is that you can't graft apple trees onto the lemon ones. Citrus is the rule. If you're going to be grafted to the Lord, you're stuck loving. You can't do it partway. You're connected. You may not look like a lemon (tangerines don't), but you're part of the same family. And we all honor the source of our life.

Now you know why we're sour sometimes.

Easter 6
John 15:9-17
by Larry Winebrenner

The Roots of Love

Esmerelda watched with disgust as Amanda's boyfriend walked around from the passenger door of the Impala and timidly kissed Amanda's cheek. Esmerelda watched as the young man slowly climbed the steps of the apartment building, looking at each step as if counting. He rang the doorbell, then turned toward Amanda and gave a shy wave. Only after he had entered the door did Amanda drive away.

"Why did you take up with that loser?" Esmerelda asked her granddaughter for the fiftieth time. "He's useless, has no job, couldn't get one, and if he got one he couldn't hold it. He doesn't have the sense God gave a billy goat."

Amanda had heard it all before. She had whittled her responses down to "He loves me, Grandma."

"I've told you before, you can't live on love. That boy will never be able to do anything meaningful for you." These were words Esmerelda would regret in days soon to come.

Amanda thought about their first encounter. Arthur had entered the flower shop where Amanda worked.

"I'm here for Miss Lily's flowers," he said.

"Do you have an order form?" she asked. He seemed confused. "Here. Let me call her," Amanda said. The order was confirmed, and Arthur took it to Miss Lily.

After several weeks, he spoke to her on the fifth errand. "Miss Mandy," he said, "you're not very good looking." That cut to the quick. No one ever asked Amanda for a date, no matter how nice she tried to be. But Arthur didn't stop there. He went on, rather shyly, "But that don't make no never mind. To me you are the most beautiful girl in the world. I love you."

He fled after saying his little speech and he never returned to the flower shop. Amanda couldn't get those words out of her head. No one had ever said anything like that to her in her whole life.

One day she saw him at church. She waited for him outside after the service. "Arthur," she called as he walked by. He looked like he was about to run. "Could we go to the movies together some day?" she asked. He really looked ready to flee.

"Miss Mandy," he said, "I can't take you to the movies. I can't drive."

"I'll drive," she said quickly. "We'll go dutch."

"What's that mean?" he asked.

"It means each of us have to pay our own way."

He thought a few minutes, then said, "That's good. I can pay for my half of the gas if we don't put too much in."

That's when she realized she really liked Arthur.

A week after Amanda had her latest discussion with her grandmother, she and Arthur attended the church picnic at Hell's Canyon Park. The park got its name from the fiercely raging stream in the bottom of a ravine in the park. Picnickers were warned to stay away from the rim of the ravine.

Still, soon after settling in, everyone heard a scream. They saw Amanda being swept downstream in Hell's Canyon River. "The cliff just caved in," sobbed a little girl.

It didn't matter how it happened. Amanda was certain to be dashed to pieces in the rapids and the series of three waterfalls downstream. Then, she miraculously grabbed a rock jutting sharply out of the water. It was a tiny miracle, but she couldn't hold on long.

"Somebody could try swimming out there with this rope and we could pull her in," said the devastated associate pastor.

"In that current?"

"If someone started far enough upstream..."

"They'd be beat up on the rocks before they reached her."

"She can't hold on for long."

While everyone else was talking, Arthur slipped the end of the rope beneath his belt, walked up to the spot from which Amanda fell, and he jumped.

"That crazy guy just jumped in with a rope!" cried a voice.

They watched him tumble, turn, get upright, swim, strike a rock, and repeat the process. Everyone held their breaths. Arthur managed to get beyond the rock Amanda was clinging to. The rope slipped over her body and threatened to go beyond her reach.

She grabbed it. The force of Arthur's body heading downstream threatened the rescue. Those above pulled mightily. Finally they saw Arthur say something to Amanda. He pulled the rope from under his belt and was swept away.

When the group was finally been able to pull Amanda ashore and help her to the top of the ravine, they asked her what Arthur's last words were. She said, "I love you."

Ascension of Our Lord
Luke 24:44-53
by Peter Andrew Smith

Witnessing to the Truth

Janine sat alone crying in the midst of the life and activity of the park. Many of the people passing by never saw her as they enjoyed the spring morning. Some of the people noticed her but turned away when they saw her tears. A small dog was drawn to the sounds of her sobs but its owner pulled it in another direction before they came too close. Janine covered her face with her hands and wept.

"Are you okay?"

Janine looked up into the face of a middle-aged woman dressed in a business suit. The woman's makeup was perfect and her clothes were crisply pressed.

"I'll move along," Janine said, wiping her cheeks and trying to gather herself together. "I didn't mean to bother anyone."

"I don't think you are bothering anyone in the least," the woman said, sitting down beside her. "Besides, the park is a good place to come when you're sad. I've cried here many a time."

"I'm not crying."

"Then why the tears?" the woman asked.

"Nothing a stranger would care about," Janine said.

"I wouldn't have asked if I didn't care. My name is Angela."

Janine introduced herself.

"Good," Angela said with a gentle smile. "Now that we're no longer strangers, why don't you tell me what brought you to the park this morning to cry."

Tears began to run down Janine's face. "My mother died last night."

"I'm sorry." Angela said.

"It's not fair," Janine said. "She was a good person, so full of energy and so caring. The cancer just took her life away. I never got the chance to say everything I wanted to say to her."

"There is never enough time in life to say everything we want to say." Angela handed Janine a tissue. "She sounds like a wonderful person."

"She was. The best mother a girl could ever want."

"Tell me about her," Angela said.

Janine began slowly telling about her mother. At first she talked about her death, the pain of seeing her withered and weak lying in the hospital bed. She told of her anger at finding out about her mother's cancer and her search for a cure. She cried as she described her mother's illness.

Then she laughed as she told of her mother's jokes about hospital food and the shameless flirting her mother did with the young male orderly who worked nights. She spoke of the times her mother took her to the zoo as a young girl and the Sunday dinners they always had after church.

"I'll never have another Sunday dinner with her," Janine said, covering her face again and sobbing.

Angela handed her another tissue when the sobbing quieted. "You know, your face lights up when you speak of your mother."

"I loved her."

"And it sounds like she loved you."

Janine nodded. "She did. No matter what I did in life she still loved me. Even when I didn't go to church I knew I was welcome at her house for dinner."

"Did your mother go to church often?"

"Every Sunday. The last thing she told me was not to be afraid, that she was going to a better place and that Jesus was looking after her," Janine said. "She wasn't afraid in the least to die."

"She sounds like a strong woman."

"She was," Janine said, nodding. "I wish I was as strong as her. I wish I had her faith."

"You have her faith," Angela said. "She shared it with you in her love for you and in the way she lived her life and the way she faced her death. She showed you her faith by telling what she believed and in teaching you about Jesus."

Janine nodded. "She always said prayer was the way through a hard time."

"Would you like to pray together?" Angela asked, extending an open hand.

The two grasped hands and together they prayed in the park, surrounded by people that spring morning. Most of the people ignored them and continued on with their lives without paying any attention to the two women speaking with God. But a few people noticed and carried with them the sight of two strangers who became friends through a tragedy and through the hope of the gospel of Jesus Christ.

Easter 7
Psalm 1; John 17:6-19
by Argile Smith

Choices

Nicole and Dana stood in a long line at the coffee shop waiting to place their orders. Friends since college, the two of them enjoyed an afternoon together whenever they could schedule it. Fifteen years had passed since they had graduated. Across those years, their relationship had grown deeper.

Not only did they enjoy each other's company, they found strength in one another that helped them through some of the tough times in each of their lives. Once, when Nicole got fired from her job, Dana kept on encouraging her not to give up on her career. Eventually Nicole got back in the game, so to speak, and from that point her career took off in a new and lucrative direction.

But Dana helped Nicole, too. Dana enjoyed a personal relationship with the Lord but Nicole didn't consider her to be a religious person. When Nicole was a little girl, she lost her mother to cancer. When she told Dana about the loss one night in their dorm room in college, she explained that she prayed every day for God to make her mom well. In her childlike way, she really believed that he would heal her. When her mom died, Nicole said that she became bitter about religion and gave up on God. She couldn't see any value in devoting herself to a deity that hadn't given any attention to her at the point of her deepest need as a child.

Saying good-bye to her mother for the last time broke Nicole's little heart. Growing up without her mom made her life unbearable at times. To make matters worse, she had to put up with her dad, who numbed his grief with alcohol and eventually became addicted to it. Throughout her years as a teenager, she had to deal with an unabated sorrow that always simmered in her soul.

Dana took advantage of every opportunity to talk with Nicole about a personal relationship with God, but so far her efforts had been in vain. Nicole constantly replied with the same rejoinder: "Dana, you know that I'm not religious. I'm not interested!" Sometimes she would add, "Dana, believing in God has been good for you but you can't make me believe that it's good for me. I've made it this far without believing and I am sure that I can take care of myself without any help from the Divine."

Dana saw an opportunity to talk with Nicole about God that afternoon as they visited each other at the coffee shop. As they stood in line, she heard Nicole make a comment about the menu posted on the coffee shop wall. As she surveyed it, Nicole commented on the number of options. As they waited in line, Nicole counted out loud the number of coffee selections. Frustrated because she couldn't make up her mind about what she wanted, she complained to Dana that she had too many choices to make. "Sometimes," she said to Dana, "I would like to have only a couple of choices."

"In fact, you do!" Dana replied. "But not necessarily when it comes to coffee."

"Are you going to get religious on me again?" Nicole replied with a hint of uneasiness and caution in her voice.

"No, not really," Dana said. "But you could take it that way."

"What do you mean?"

"Well, everyone everywhere has really only two paths to choose from when it comes to how we will live. Either we take the path that has us living according to God's ways, or we'll choose another way. But one fact is certain. You've got to make a choice."

"I've already made my choice. I want to live without God. I don't need him."

"That's your choice but have you stopped to think about what taking that path means to you?"

"Yes, it means I won't ever be disappointed!" groused Nicole, still stinging as an adult because God didn't answer her prayer when she was a child.

"Yes, you will. You'll be disappointed with yourself because you didn't give God a chance. Rest assured that he doesn't feel about you the way you feel about him."

"Maybe you've got a point," Nicole said.

The author of Psalm 1 described the difference the choices would make in a person's life. As he prayed for his disciples, Jesus asked the Father to guide them so they would choose well (John 17:6-19).

Pentecost Sunday
Acts 2:1-21
by W. Lamar Massingill

God's Spirit Changes Us

They are the worst words I have ever seen, and the biggest marketing lie ever: "easy to assemble." After reading the instructions I know that unless I have a degree in architectural engineering I'm in for a rough evening.

Joyce and I almost separated (well, not really, but it felt like it!) in 1994 over an "easy to assemble" Christmas tree, as after hours of trying, I finally said in defeat, "I ain't doing this no more."

Then by 2001 things had changed. We purchased an "easy to assemble" crystal cabinet and paid our son $200 to come and put the darn thing together! I guess we realized that things are easy to assemble for those with a strong left brain for nuts and bolts but not so easy when you don't have your certification in nuts-and-bolts architecture.

Human beings aren't that easy to assemble, either. In fact, without the breath of God we cannot grow into full humanness, the kind that Jesus modeled. And what exactly is the breath of God? Whether it is the Hebrew word *ruachhi* or the Greek word *pneuma*, both are translated as "spirit" or "breath."

What happened at the high festival time in Jerusalem recorded in Acts 2 was genuinely dramatic, as the Holy Spirit or the Holy "breath" of God came upon them. This was what Jesus had promised his people before he was crucified — that there would be a "comforter" to be within them on the journey, the last thing his people would need to be "spiritually assembled" and ready for the journey of a lifetime.

We human beings can no more live fully without spirit than we can without breath. It's no wonder these two words are simultaneously translated from the Greek *pneuma*. Sadly, many do not recognize their own breath or spirit as a gift from the holy one that has the power to change them into the fullest of human beings.

This brings me to one of the effects of this dramatic occasion that means more to me than any other: the change that had happened in the disciple whose name was Peter.

His story is among the most dramatic in Holy Scripture. Peter was literally the one who set the interpretive word, not only around the event of Pentecost but also around the early church. He was so brave and courageous in the words he spoke. He was the one who emerged as the true leader of the Jerusalem church.

Peter was not always the tower of strength you see and hear in these passages about the coming of the Holy Spirit and the consequent formation of the early church. It is sometimes assumed — and I think wrongly so — that impressive characters are born rather than made. One way of evading our responsibility is to come to the simple conclusion that "some people got it and some don't." Therefore, we think there is nothing one can do about one's self. However, such fatalism finds no support in the life story of this man who was called Peter.

When we first encounter Simon Peter, he is anything but strong and stable. In fact, he was one who could oscillate between poles of good and bad faster than any of the disciples. This is pretty much the kind of person Jesus first encountered in Peter. He was emotional, impulsive, and erratic. No figure in all of scripture was given to more violence, betrayal, and fatalism than Simon Peter. He could rise higher more rapidly and then fall lower just as rapidly as anyone you could imagine. He could at one moment be uttering words that were nothing short of revelations from God, then the very next minute be sounding like Satan himself.

The old Simon Peter was an incarnation of Saint Paul's statement that "the spirit is willing, but the flesh is weak." Something obviously happened between the time of Peter's broken beginnings with Jesus and the emergence of the tower of faith and strength we see in the Acts of the Apostles.

I believe that as we grow and experience pain, emptiness, and hopelessness, and feel as cut off as Peter did after he had betrayed Jesus, God starts breathing. God starts "spiriting," if you will. The result of that is that Peter received all the things he needed to make a difference in the lives of others.

I once had a professor in divinity school who used to say, "Only life can change life." That is, when another life touches us in spiritual ways, we are inspired, in-breathed, or in-spirited; the very word that is literally translated "breath."

God breathes on us daily. God gives of his life and spirit to us daily. And like Peter and the multitude there on that dramatic day in Jerusalem, we find that when the spirit of truth comes to us we discover to our surprise (God's other name) a new life and boldness, and we stand up, a vast multitude who are called the church.

Holy Trinity Sunday
Isaiah 6:1-8
by Frank Ramirez

The Radiant Life

I'm a sucker for old books and I'm glad I'm not the only one. It can be lonely believing you're the only one who appreciates a particular vice.

Old books are like snapshots. Everyone assumes that their era is in some way the apex, the culmination, the ancient, and the ultimate. Time moves on. There we are, staring out of our yearbook pages, and it's not a pretty sight. Old books preserve the past mercilessly.

My friend down the road, Farmer Bob, is a sucker for a deal, and most times he's got a sharp eye for a bargain. But the other day he bit off more than he could chew; so he left behind a little for me to munch on as well.

Basically, he bid on boxes of books at an auction, not realizing that the reason books go for so little is that they aren't worth much. Unlike fine wine and antiques, they don't always wear so well.

My son Jacob, fourteen years old and twice my size, rode off in Bob's truck to pick up the books, and as a reward (and just because I'm a good sport) he left behind two boxes of books for my pleasure.

Some of the books can't be beat: *Financial Strategies for the '80s*; volume one of an old travel guide, reflecting the world before the fall of the Berlin Wall; *The Hangup Handbook* from *Cosmopolitan*, designed to help young women get with "it," whatever "it" is; a cautionary book about the future of brain control.

Most of the books are good for a laugh, and even worth saving to use as gag gifts. But one book I pulled out of the stack proved memorable. I thought I'd get a nice chuckle at its naivete, but the joke was on me. I couldn't put the book down — it was well-written; it was about an interesting subject; I cared.

The book was about a radiant life. That's what it said on the cover: *The Radiant Life of Vera B. Blinn*. Radiant. The chapters are prefaced by inspirational poems, sometimes florid and overwrought, short on images and long on tired rhymes. And the author is identified as Mrs. J. Hal Smith. Who knows what her real name was?

It is a little volume with faded purple cloth over cardboard covers. A blank page on the inside proclaims it is the property of Ruth Swank. There are 27 names written in Ruth's neat handwriting. "Please read," she wrote inside. "Put X after your name and pass on to someone else." Ruth thought it was that important. So did her friends. Each of those 27 names had an X next to it. They all read the book.

It was published in 1921, a scant year after Vera Blinn's death following a brief thirty years of life. During those thirty years she failed to achieve her goal. But her life shines brightly on these aging pages.

1890-1920. A young woman called to the ministry who never considered herself a minister. Working her way through college, working at the denominational level of the United Brethren (before they merged with the Methodists), high school and college teacher, magazine editor, and founder of missionary societies. Her speeches could shake down some serious money from a crowd to support missions. She was on fire. People couldn't resist her.

The biography constantly alludes to her sharp sense of humor, her bright attitude, as well as to a darker side — unnamed sins and imperfections that make the portrayal believable.

She dreamed of going to the mission fields. That was the great goal of her life. Like Isaiah in this scripture passage,

Vera Blinn clearly heard God's call to ministry. And just as clearly she replied, "Here I am. Send me."

It never happened. She contracted diabetes and died unexpectedly before she could accomplish all her goals. So was her life a failure? I don't think so. Her hard work inspired others to take God's word to the four corners of the world. Her own willingness to go clearly pleased God. More clearly, she accomplished a greater goal. These are the words from her notebook printed at the head of the chapter titled "Her Crowning":

Think of
Stepping on shore and finding it heaven!
Of taking hold of a hand and finding it God's hand;
Of breathing a new air and finding it Celestial air;
Of feeling invigorated and finding it immortality;
Of passing from storm and tempest to an unknown calm;
Of waking up and finding it home!

So much for the superior attitude. And the book made me think.

There are many stars that don't fit into the constellations when we look out at the night sky, many stars whose names don't immediately come to mind. Go out to the country, get away from the city light, and those faint stars fill the heavens and turn the night into day.

Most of the star shadows are too faint to be seen, unless you're looking. Most of the tombstones are too faded to be read, unless you bend over. Time passes, and lives are swallowed whole and the memories of the memories grow dim.

As the past fades it is swallowed in the great noise of the static, all the talking, all the crying, all the breathing, all the living, all the shifting of weight, all the lifting, and all the toting. The great mass of information makes everything knowable and nothing knowable. There is simply too much — too many people, too many events.

So every light that shines in the darkness, every noise that pierces the static, every pressed memory that slips from between the pages is a reminder that there is a great dance, a marvelous hand-holding, a walking forward and a walking back again, that we all have our part for a moment or a day, and all the others, all the radiant lives, all the memorable and forgotten people, have their part too.

Vera B. Blinn is part of that cloud of witnesses spoken about in scripture. She heard God's call: "Whom shall I send?" How many of us are as ready as her to answer, no matter what the cost, "Here I am. Send me!"

Proper 5 / Pentecost 2 / Ordinary Time 10
2 Corinthians 4:13—5:1
by Keith Hewitt

Marathon

"You're Mrs. Mueller — Dora Mueller — aren't you?"

Dora Mueller glanced toward the person who'd spoken, cocking her head slightly to bring her good ear to bear. "That's right," she agreed, barely pausing as she made her way across the church parking lot; she was making pretty good time this morning and did not want to break her momentum. The pain in her knees and hips was a manageable six or seven, instead of the screaming nine or ten that it often was this time of year — perhaps the new combination of anti-inflammatory and painkillers really was helping.

The speaker fell in beside her as she walked. They walked in near silence, except for the metallic click of her cane as she brought it forward and leaned on it with every other step and the sound of her own breathing — labored, with little gasps puffing out when she stepped down on her right foot. "Do I know you?" she asked after they had crossed half the lot.

"No, not really. But I've heard a lot about you. You're pretty active here."

"Hardly," she grunted. "It's been a lot of years since I was 'pretty active' anywhere."

"You play the organ every week, and you still run the Women's Auxiliary." It wasn't a question.

She gave a dismissive wave with her free hand and winced as a needle of pain shot through her wrist. "That's an hour a week, plus two meetings a month and whatever weddings or funerals come our way," she countered. "That's not very active."

"And you do Sunday school."

"I don't teach it anymore — gave that up awhile ago, so it's just another hour a week. If you've ever been to class, you know it's a pretty social time, not too strenuous." She turned her head toward the stranger again, eyes narrowed. "You haven't been, have you? I don't remember you."

"No — I've sat in on a few services, but not Sunday school."

They were at the entrance to the Fellowship Hall now — the lower level of the church building. The stranger stepped ahead of her hastily, opened the door, and held it for her as she entered the building. "So tell me," the stranger asked as she passed by, "what's been your favorite thing to do over the years?"

She paused inside the door and swept over the stranger with bright, curious eyes. "Now that's a pretty peculiar question, if you don't mind me saying so. Who are you, and why are you asking?"

The answering smile was enough to wipe away any concerns she might have had. "What's that old saying? I'm just a friend you haven't met yet," the stranger answered. "But to tell you the honest truth, you're kind of well known back where I come from, and I wanted to know more about you — just talk to you for a bit this morning."

She peered at the stranger for another heartbeat or two, then snorted and shook her head "I guess Warhol was right — everybody does get fifteen minutes of fame." She shook her head. "Well known."

"So how long have you been going to church?"

"Oh, I don't know. After my daughter was born — that would make it about fifty years I guess." She nodded toward the stairs to the sanctuary, started toward them after the stranger followed her gesture, then began to walk with her. They mounted two steps to get to the foot of the first flight of stairs. Dora paused just long enough to eye the steps and get a better grip on her cane, then grabbed the handrail and began to pull herself up slowly; she did not notice the stranger's hand on her elbow, helping to steady her as she climbed with fragile determination, equal parts Mother Teresa and Sir Edmund Hillary.

"I know about the organ, and the Women's Auxiliary. What else have you done?"

She shrugged — a motion that caused sharp pain to radiate from her shoulder to her elbow; she ignored it, refusing to give it space in her mind. "Nothing much, I guess. We did a few mission trips early on — stopped that after my husband was killed in a car accident. Helped organize the food pantry, did some outreach work, taught Sunday school to the little ones." She paused halfway up the first flight, her expression wistful. "I think I liked that the most. I taught little ones for almost twenty years. They were so full of questions and so eager to learn — so accepting of what we tried to teach them." She looked at the stranger, nodded, and said, "They may not understand the theology, but they get the idea of grace, and they get forgiveness, and they understand that God loves them. I think that's a pretty good start."

The stranger smiled again. "I agree. And you'd be surprised how many of those youngsters kept what you taught them in their heart and used it later in life."

She sighed. "I like to think so." She shrugged again, winced, and took a tighter grip on the railing, pulling herself up the next step. People would be coming soon and she wanted to be ready to play.

"If you don't mind my asking, what kept you going all those years?" The stranger nodded toward the rest of the stairs in the first flight, and the half-dozen stairs on the next. "What makes you climb these stairs every week?"

Her eyebrows drew together and she said, "Well, I like the people here — it's like a family. A couple of generations of family, all under one roof." Reach, step up, rest. Reach, step up…

"And that's enough to make you face these stairs every week? That's enough to get you out of bed early on a Sunday morning?"

She considered this, then shook her head slowly. "No, not really." Reach, step up, rest. Reach… "When the arthritis got really bad, I used to think about cutting back. I hated these stairs. And then one Easter it hit me — I was sitting at the organ listening to the scripture, and it hit me: Jesus let himself go through everything he did, and then he carried his own cross up the hill to the place where they would kill him. And he did it for us. I figure if he can carry that cross up a hill, I can carry this tired old body up some stairs." Reach, step up, rest. "I guess my whole life here is kind of like that. I found Jesus here — really found him. And he did so much for me — he healed my soul, brought me back to God, and I realized I had to tell people about that any way I could. Whatever little bit I do isn't a big deal, but I've got to do something. I owe him that."

As she spoke her heart beat faster — whether from the effort of climbing the steps or the urgency to make this stranger understand what Jesus meant to her, she couldn't tell. She took a deep breath, then a deeper one. She was not used to talking while she climbed — it was making her winded. They were at the landing between flights — only half a dozen more stairs to go. She leaned against the wall, breathing heavily, and eyed the stairs.

Half a dozen, but they looked like they were carved into the side of Mount Everest. The stranger had paused, and she took advantage of the chance to rest a bit more before finishing.

The stranger's smile was like some magical heat lamp — it seemed to reach to her very core and warm her from the inside out. "Dora, I want you to know that everything you've done here is significant. You've helped bring people to Jesus — don't ever doubt that."

"Okay," she said slowly, almost doubtfully.

"Look, why don't you rest for a minute," the stranger said, patting one of the stairs. "You've got time." Dora started to shake her head, then suddenly realized that it seemed like a good idea... a very good idea. Gingerly, holding herself up with the cane in one hand and the other on the railing, she lowered herself to the second step and slumped. Relief radiated out through her body, except for that pain in her arm again. She flexed her hand and rested her head against the railing.

The stranger was talking again; she opened her eyes, looking at him without turning her head. "Dora, I know it's been hard for you but you didn't stop, and even though your body was wearing out your spirit just grew stronger."

"I suppose that's true." Her voice was faint now.

"I know it is," the stranger said gently. "Now rest — you've climbed enough stairs."

The stranger's touch was soft, and the warmth of it enveloped her like a cocoon. She resisted but a moment, then let herself go... let herself rest. The pain faded away, replaced by something new... something wonderful that seemed to lift her skyward.

In due time, the watchful stranger reached out once more and closed her eyes.

She would not need them to see the wonders that awaited...

Proper 6 / Pentecost 3 / Ordinary Time 11
Mark 4:26-34
by Peter Andrew Smith

The Kingdom of God Is Like This...

"Is everything okay?" Tad asked from the hallway.

"What do you mean?" Reverend Latesha said as she looked up from proofreading the weekly church bulletin.

"I mean with our group being cancelled today."

"Oh," she replied, "Roger has the flu."

Latesha was not really surprised that one of the boys from the after-school program at the church was concerned that it was cancelled, but she was quite surprised that it was Tad who showed up at her door. Tad had never spoken more than a "hello" to her before today, although he was always at the program. She knew he lived with his grandmother, but he never came to church with her except at Christmas and Easter and then, by the look on his face, under protest.

"Is Roger going to be okay?"

"Sure, he's just sick today," Latesha said. "Nothing to worry about. He hopes to be here tomorrow."

"Oh."

She went back to what she had been doing, but didn't get very far before she realized that Tad was still standing in the doorway.

"Was there anything else, Tad?" she asked.

"Um," he said, "I just wanted to tell you that I really enjoy the after-school program."

"I'm glad. Roger always tells me that he looks forward to seeing all of you. And things are certainly active when you get busy in the gym."

"Yeah, sorry about the window. Gran said some people were upset about it."

She smiled. "The trustees were, but I think they also remembered how things are when an indoor soccer game gets going. The fact that you offered to pay for the window helped, too."

"Some of us are worried that the church will stop letting us come here after school."

Reverend Latesha closed her laptop and motioned Tad to have a seat in her office.

"The board hasn't made any decisions but there is a review going on of everything happening at the church."

"So we might not be able to come here anymore?"

"Tad, I don't know what the board will decide. With Roger leaving at the end of December to go back to school, it's hard to know what we'll do in January."

Tad pulled at his shirt nervously. "Will someone else make sure we get to come here after school?"

"I don't know."

"Because some of us don't have anywhere else to go but an empty house," Tad said. "Roger has made this place a home for us. And not just for the kids from this church."

"What do you mean?"

"Well, when Singh's sister was hit by the car we all prayed for her, and we went to help out at the store so his mother could stay with her."

Reverend Latesha knew that the program was open to everyone in the neighborhood. She also knew about the prayers after the accident because Roger had asked her for an appropriate prayer to use with the teens since the Singhs were Muslim. But she didn't know about the teens helping out at the local corner store.

"And this is somewhere where we learn more about God together," Tad continued.

"That's what we do at church on Sunday," Reverend Latesha said.

"Yeah, but a lot of us have questions and when we get together we are able to talk and Roger sometimes tells us about the Bible too."

She nodded. Roger had been in her office more than once about the difficulties he was having introducing a Bible study to the teens.

"Um," Tad said, "we didn't know Roger was sick, so most of us are here."

Reverend Latesha smiled. "I know. That's why I opened up the gym. I'm around this afternoon so you can shoot baskets and hang out if you want. You saw the sign, didn't you?"

"Yeah. We were reading about King Saul yesterday and how he broke his word to God."

"That's an interesting story and I bet there was a lot of discussion around it."

"Yeah." Tad got up but didn't go past the doorway.

"Was there something else, Tad?" Reverend Latesha asked before she opened her laptop again.

"Since you are here and you're the minister and all, some of us were wondering," Tad said, pulling at his shirt again, "could you lead the Bible study today?"

She looked at the paperwork sitting on her desk. "Give me ten minutes to finish up what I was doing and I'll meet you in the hall."

"Awesome!" Tad said as he raced off.

Reverend Latesha sat at her desk for a few minutes, thinking about the conversation that had just taken place. She was one of the people who had been skeptical when Roger asked permission to start the after-school program. She recognized after it got going that there was value to it but hadn't argued for it to continue at the last board meeting. Like the rest of the board, she felt the church's time and money should be spent on a more religious program for young people. She picked up the phone and dialed the number of the chair of the church board.

"Simon, can you drop by the church this afternoon? Good. I think that the answer as to how to reach the young people with the gospel has been happening right here without us realizing."

Proper 7 / Pentecost 4 / Ordinary Time 12
Mark 4:35-41
by C. David McKirachan

Passing Over to the Other Side

I love to sail. People who like powerboats or anything else that has a steering wheel that you can turn in a specific direction and thus direct the vehicle in question have no use for sailboats or sailors. We can point our boats all we want but the wind is our master. A sailor is not in the business of going somewhere; a sailor is just in the business of going.

I have wasted most of my life in the vain pursuit of goals. I will be kind to myself and lay a lot of the blame for this useless chase on our culture. "Measureable" and "attainable" are two of the stupidest words in our language. They were devised by people who either have no understanding of life or who have a really sick sense of humor. Nothing of any import is either measurable or attainable. It gets really crazy when the church begins using these words. Sometimes I wonder why God doesn't fry us.

Sailing reminds us of Heisenberg, who with enough objective proof to choke the proverbial dinosaur demonstrated that objectivity is impossible. Anytime we observe something we change it. So much for objective reality. So how can we ever choose a direction and go there? Winnie the Pooh had it right — he said life is a "long explore." We aren't called to solve it or accomplish it or even arrive. We're called to put up our sails and see what happens.

A lot changed during that storm. But the most important thing was that the disciples recognized Jesus for who he really was. During the most difficult transitions of my life, I need to remember that the most important thing I can accomplish is recognizing who he really is — and that no matter what I think, he's in the boat with me.

My boat's name is *Norma Jean.*

Proper 8 / Pentecost 5 / Ordinary Time 13
Psalm 130
by John Sumwalt

A Deep Longing

We have been shopping for a new door for the garage that adjoins our 94-year-old farmhouse in southwest Wisconsin. The door came apart in my hands the last time I was trying to close it, leaving a six-inch wide gap at the bottom. This happened just as we were loading the car for the two-and-one-half-hour drive back to our city lives in Milwaukee, so I didn't take time to board up the opening. During the two weeks before we returned to mow the grass and have some much-needed R & R, I worried that someone or something might crawl through the breech and wreak havoc. Our ravenous raccoon neighbors and the woodchucks who claim squatters' rights in the backyard are notorious for destroying things that are precious to us.

When we arrived two nights ago, I was relieved to discover that everything seemed to be as I had left it. About an hour later, when I stepped into the garage to get a garden tool, an emaciated calico cat with an inch-wide wound around the center of her tail strode out from behind the stairs that lead up to the laundry room and gave me a "where have you been?" look. It was as if she belonged there and had been waiting impatiently for us to come home. Since we had never met I was not only startled by her presence, I was puzzled by this look of familiarity.

Just as I was about to call Jo to come quickly and see what I had found in the garage, two six-week-old kittens scrambled out from behind the cots we keep stored under the stairs for guests. It was love at first sight when Jo got a look at those kittens. And I have to confess, I was just as smitten. I ran into the house to get a bowl of milk and a can of tuna fish. The next day when I went in to town I stopped at cousin Chet's Seed & Feed and picked up a 20-lb. bag of cat food.

The kittens shied away from us at first but the mama cat came right up and rubbed boldly against my leg as if we belonged to each other. Clearly she had belonged to someone before her single-parent life in our garage. She purred when I knelt down to pet her — and then when I pulled my hand away after a few moments she let out a plaintive meow like I have never heard from any cat before. It seemed to come from the depths of her cat being. I felt in her cry a deep longing that moved me deeply. There was in that sound something I have known in my own times of distress, both what Paul called the "sigh too deep for words" and that long, anxiety-releasing sigh of relief that comes when an unbearable burden has been lifted.

Could it be that we were an answer to prayer? Does the Lord of the universe pay attention to the supplications of cats?

Proper 9 / Pentecost 6 / Ordinary Time 14
Mark 6:1-13
by Peter Andrew Smith

Out in Faith

"Are you sure about this?" Thomas asked as he looked at the bus schedule again.

"Yes," Philip said.

"But we have no real plan, no money, and nowhere to stay."

Philip sighed. "We're going to the inner city to preach about Jesus and to help out in community projects. You knew that when you agreed to come along."

"Yes, but I expected that we would have a detailed plan, a budget to guide us, and maybe that we would be part of a larger group of people. I mean, what do we do when we get there?"

"You saw the pictures of the vandalism and the devastation. I don't think we'll have any problem finding something to do."

Thomas rolled his eyes. "Okay maybe, but where do we stay? People are sleeping in the streets there and we don't have any money."

Philip shrugged. "Then we will sleep on the streets too."

"But…"

"The bus is leaving soon and I'm getting on it," Philip said, picking up his backpack and starting toward the door. "Are you going to come with me or not?"

"Do I have a choice? I'm not letting you go alone." Thomas grabbed his bag and guitar case. He fell in line behind Philip and climbed onto the bus. There weren't many people heading their way, so they had no problem getting a seat together and finding a spot for their bags.

Thomas shifted in his seat a number of times before turning to Philip. "What happens if they don't want us where we are going?"

Philip rubbed his forehead and closed his eyes. "Then I guess we move along to the next neighborhood."

Thomas chewed his lower lip. "How will we know when it is time to go home?"

"The same way we knew it was time to go help in the inner city."

"What? That's no answer."

Philip opened his eyes and turned toward Thomas. "What do you want from me?"

"Answers, certainties, plans."

"We are going to the inner city because it is an area that needs people willing to volunteer. We're going together because you have carpentry experience and can play the guitar, and I can do some plumbing and electrical and am comfortable preaching. We know there is lots to do," Philip said. "We both saw pictures of what the place is like."

"I know all of that. I want you to answer the questions about what I don't know," Thomas said, "like what's going to happen when we get there, what we will be doing, and whether we're going to make any difference."

Philip shrugged. "No idea."

"Then why in heaven's name are we going?"

"To help people who need help. To tell people about Jesus."

"But why us? Why you and me?"

"Because there is no reason we can't."

"But there is so much we don't know about what we are doing," Thomas said. "This doesn't make sense. Why are we doing this? Nothing is certain about this trip. I mean that makes this whole thing an act of…"

"... faith?" Philip said.

Thomas opened his mouth and then closed it. He stared straight ahead for a while before finally closing his eyes. His lips moved slightly for a few moments and he settled back into his seat. He and Philip sat in silence while the few passengers worked their way onto the bus and the departure time arrived.

The bus driver came down the aisle asking everyone for their tickets. Thomas handed them to her.

Her face scrunched up as she read their destination. "You boys realize that area is pretty bad?"

They both nodded.

"Do you know what you are getting yourself into? You can get your money back on these tickets but once I punch them there are no refunds," she said. "Are you sure about this?"

"Yes," Thomas answered, before Philip could say anything.

Proper 10 / Pentecost 7 / Ordinary Time 15
2 Samuel 6:1-5, 12b-19
by Frank Ramirez

Now That's Scary!

> The anger of the Lord was kindled against Uzzah; and God struck him there because he reached out his hand to the ark; and he died there beside the ark of God.
> — 2 Samuel 6:7

I suspect everyone had special fears when they were younger. If we're lucky we outgrow those fears.

One of my great fears when I was young was army ants. There were no army ants living within thousands and thousands of miles of me, but that didn't matter. I'd seen the devastation they'd leave behind after rushing through an area on a documentary when I was very young, and the images didn't leave me. As I lay in bed at night I was sure the rustling of the grass outside my window was the arrival of millions of army ants who would shortly overwhelm me and leave behind nothing but a few bones before scurrying on their way.

By the way, I was also afraid of a strange series of folds in the curtain of my bedroom that reminded me of Frankenstein's face glaring down at me. And there were other fears as well.

But one of the most frightening things I endured as a child was this particular story. As a child, I was appalled when I came upon the story of Uzzah and the Ark of the Covenant.

It was so unfair. More important, I knew if I'd have been standing there in Uzzah's place, I'd have put out my hand to right the Ark. I would have expected to be rewarded for it.

Big headlines: LOCAL BOY SAVES ARK OF THE COVENANT FROM FALLING! Congratulations from my parents and teachers and the admiration of my friends.

But I would have died if I'd have touched it! Now that's frightening.

The story, as we have it in 2 Samuel 6, may be simply told. King David unified the northern and southern kingdoms and conquered Jerusalem to make it his own District of Columbia. In an effort to make his capital secure, he prepared to take the Ark of the Covenant to the holy city. There was great singing and dancing. Suddenly the Ark began to fall. Uzzah, reacting as most of us would, reached out to prevent this terrible calamity. For his pains, he was struck dead.

When I asked questions about this story I was told the whole matter was a "mystery." We students quickly learned that "mystery," when applied to God, was a synonym for "Shut up, if you know what's good for you." We would understand mysteries, we were told, in the next life. For now we had to accept them.

I couldn't accept this story. Uzzah did what I would have done. I just knew it. Here I was, eight years old, and I would have been as dead as he. Who wouldn't put a hand out to protect the Ark?

Things change. Now that I'm older, when I come before the throne of grace I come willingly — but also with just a little caution. We sometimes forget that while God is good, he is also dangerous — in the same way that electricity is dangerous. One day an otherwise careful lineman may neglect to remove his wedding ring, make a mistake, and get electrocuted. There is no appeal to such an instant death.

Strange to say, it is dangerous to get too close to God. It is also good beyond words to do so.

Proper 11 / Pentecost 8 / Ordinary Time 16
Mark 6:30-34, 53-56
by C. David McKirachan

Living with Pain

I grew up in the manse — my father was a preacher and a pastor. My brother went the same way. You'd think after all that genetic and experiential momentum plus a wonderful seminary education (go SFTS), I would have been prepared for just about anything. But I'll tell you right here, I wasn't ready for the pain.

I was not ready for the pain of young people trapped in bodies they don't recognize, struggling to be individuals, to be adult, to be successful while they are desperate to be loved and accepted and respected while all those things conflict. Whew.

I wasn't ready for the pain of married couples who start out with such high hopes and then run into the quiet isolation and desperate anger and overwhelming fatigue of family life.

I wasn't ready for the pain of lonely old age, when valuable people find themselves entrapped by limitation and hopelessness and marginalization.

My first church was in the inner city. All those people needing so many different things — coming to the sanctuary, the safe place, the church, to me, wanting something; they didn't even know what.

Sometimes they curled up and whimpered, sometimes they attacked, sometimes they put on a good show, sometimes they medicated themselves, but they were all in pain, all in need, all like sheep without a shepherd. And I? I was a kid — a kid with too much empathy for my own good. I tried, but I always felt like a failure. There was never enough...

and so often they didn't even want what I knew how to give. Whew.

I still feel their pain, these people given to me, trusting me, trusting the church to touch them in their pain, to heal them, to give them something that is more important than all the tawdry promises that have let them down. I still feel their pain, but I don't bleed like I used to. They've taught me — all these desperate people taught me.

They taught me that the only hope any of us have is not in the capability or strength of any of us. There are no solutions to our pain. But there is the miracle of compassion. There are people who care, who appreciate, who are willing to stand beside us and value us, even in our brokenness.

I wonder sometimes how Jesus put up with it. He could heal. He could cast out demons. He held the way, the truth, and the life in his bones. But he could only do so much — even with all that power and wisdom and perspective, he was limited in what he could accomplish. But he had compassion. It changed their pain, and I'm sure his as well. I hope so. It's a wonderful gift. It changes our pain into glory. Whew.

Proper 12 / Pentecost 9 / Ordinary Time 17
John 6:1-21
by W. Lamar Massingill

The Lad's Miracle of Sharing

I wonder if this episode in the life of our Lord would have ever happened had it not been for the one whom Saint John called "the lad," which is basically a child. We really don't know whether it was a small boy or girl. Most probably in that culture it was a small boy.

Have you ever thought about the attitudes and feelings the boy with the lunch had? Jewish mothers packed lunches before any of their family went on any kind of trip. It was their custom. So my guess would be that there was enough food that was fresh in more lunch packs than we know in that multitude — but not enough willingness to share it. I can almost hear the mother say before they left, "Now remember, and share!"

I'm sure the boy had some reluctance to relinquish his lunch into the hands of these mysterious others. Also, it was his lunch, packed with care and love for him to eat, and nobody else. Probably above every other hesitation was that of the "how" question, which even a child could see. "Even if I give my lunch to these others," he must have thought, "how does he expect to feed all these people with so little as I have to give?" It was a good question and he would return home that day with the answer indelibly stamped upon his memory.

What I am suggesting is the fact that it is very possible that so many others were moved by the boy's actions that they were inspired to share their meals as well. It honestly very well could have been. And to me, it would be no less a miracle: people sharing together in order that everyone may have enough food. Can you even chew on that thought a while? If we all shared of our power and abundance so that everybody would have enough to live, the church (not to mention our world) would be revitalized in a way that we have never experienced before. Right now it's not likely in our culture, where the anxiety of accomplishment and the arrogance of possessiveness run down the gutters of our greed like slimy ditch water. For present Americans, there never seems to be enough. We have not caught the great change that a miracle of sharing could bring about.

I think there were two miracles that day. One, of course, was the miracle of feeding the people. But possibly more important than that, there was a miracle of the child's sharing, without which the miracle of feeding would never have been. I hope you can hear the words of Jesus ringing in your ears: "Unless you become as children, you shall not enter into the kingdom of heaven."

My point in this story, I hope, is obvious: the boy's action of sharing should be the church's action as well. So when we ask how the church can grow, which we seem always to be asking, please remember that each individual follower of Jesus is the church. A more appropriate question then would be: "How can I grow?" All it takes is a few people to seriously ask that question and be serious about answering it. And no doubt, the miracle of sharing as the boy and Jesus shared would be part of our answer.

Proper 13 / Pentecost 10 / Ordinary Time 18
Psalm 51:1-12; John 6:24-35
by Argile Smith

No Substitutes

Eddie had to depend on his mom for literally everything in his life. Extremely disabled since birth because of cerebral palsy, he could do almost nothing for himself. He couldn't walk, feed himself, clothe himself, or even wash his face. To make matters worse for him, he couldn't utter words in a way that anyone other than his family could understand. His dad pitched in at every opportunity to help him, and his brothers and sisters helped out as well, but his mom shouldered the lion's share of responsibility for his care.

Every day of his life found him waiting in his bed for his mother to get him up and take him to the bathroom. Then she fed him his breakfast and got him dressed for the day. Throughout the day he never got very far away from her. Periodically she stopped what she was doing just to check on him. She routinely changed the channel on the television for him so he could watch his favorite programs and she gave him a snack or something to drink whenever he wanted it. She gave him his lunch and his dinner every day and she got him ready for bed every night. After she tucked him in, she kissed him on his forehead and told him that she loved him.

She also took time to sit with him and talk whenever she got a chance. She carried on a conversation with him on a variety of topics interesting to him. She asked him what he was thinking, discussed the news with him, and speculated with him about the characters on the soap opera he enjoyed watching every day. While she talked, she stroked his head or arm with her kind and gentle hand.

Because of her care, Eddie handled his disability with tremendous maturity. He took things in stride and laughter came easy to him. He loved to hear a joke but he favored good-natured repartee with his siblings and his dad.

The family doctor said that Eddie wouldn't live very long — his body had too many obstacles to overcome. He couldn't grow normally because of problems with his disability and before long his vital organs would be affected in a negative way.

But Eddie defied the doctor's prognosis. He made it to adulthood, much to everyone's surprise. Thanks to his mother's care, he lived into adulthood and he even became a member of AARP!

When he turned fifty, however, his life turned upside-down when his mom was diagnosed with cancer. For a couple of years she worked hard to fight off the disease with chemotherapy and radiation treatments. But in due time, her body gave up the fight.

Eddie handled her death with remarkable courage. He had come to see that she wouldn't survive the disease that had crept into her body. Somehow he had prepared himself for the inevitable loss of the person who made his life worth living.

Before she died, his mother made arrangements for one of Eddie's sisters to care for him. She chose well, because Eddie's new guardian had the same caring ways that characterized his mother. She took excellent care of Eddie in the years to come. Just like his mom, she got him up every day and followed the same routine, tending to every detail so his life would continue to be enriched.

Eddie appreciated what his sister did for him. He always showed his gratitude to her for the way she devoted so much of her precious time to his care. Because of her sacrifice, Eddie continued to experience the warm, personal touch that had been reflected in his relationship with his mom. He lacked for nothing, enjoyed everything just like before, and lived with the complete assurance that nothing in his life would change.

Yet something had indeed changed. Eddie's mom was absent.

When friends and family members visited Eddie after his mom's death, he always wanted to talk about her and about how much he missed her. As much as his sister tried to do everything his mom would have done for him, she still wasn't his mom. No amount of her care could change that hard fact. Nobody could substitute for his mom. He longed to see her again in heaven and he yearned for an opportunity to talk with her one more time. Nobody could take away his longing for her.

David yearned exclusively for God (Psalm 51:1-12); Jesus taught his disciples that he alone was the sole source of authentic life (John 6:24-35). No substitutes will satisfy our longing for a relationship with the Lord.

Proper 14 / Pentecost 11 / Ordinary Time 19
Psalm 130
by David O. Bales

The Final Robert

Everything seemed strange. The church was long and dark, and from the back it was difficult to see in the subdued light. The extreme strangeness began with the first speaker.

"When the final Robert was the original Bobby we had to play his games. At anyone else's birthday he was always last to come to the table; and if we were going somewhere for someone else's birthday, we had to sit and wait for him until Dad blew the horn a couple times."

Other people spoke, and then Aunt Virginia. Didn't she die ten years ago? "We gave the final Robert all the chances we gave others — the hugs and presents, and we listened to his childhood concerns. Yet he was the child of the permanent scowl and the word 'No.' "

His sister again: "When he was an adult and married, we knew the final Robert didn't like his nieces and nephews. At Christmas, our only family gathering, he didn't talk much. He would read a book instead of playing games or bundle up and go for a walk alone no matter how cold it was. We weren't surprised when one December his wife phoned to tell us that the two-hour drive at the Christmas season was just too much for them."

A colleague stood. "All teachers had to take their turn in organizing transportation and lodging for band trips. It fell to the final Robert to arrange all details for the band to travel to the state playoffs that our boys' basketball team was in. He sent notes home with band members that the buses would leave at 7 a.m. That morning he had everyone on the buses and was looking at his watch and the clipboard with the names of the band members. At 7:00 he turned to the driver and said, 'Go.' The band director beside him said, 'There's a student yet to come.' 'No matter,' final Robert said, 'It's seven on the nose.' As the buses drove out of the school's parking lot, a car rushed in, honking. The student's mother waved from the car window. The final Robert said, 'They're late. Keep going,' which the driver did. The student's mother missed a day's work and drove three hours to the game. Throughout the high school the final Robert was understood to be bad news and one who liked to deliver it."

Gladys spoke. Although often in the marriage she was quiet or uncommunicative, breaking into tears instead of being able to explain herself, today she pronounced every word correctly and spoke in full sentences. "I saw the final Robert try, but never very long. A few times he seemed even to admit his mistakes, but soon found ways to blame them on others. He gave little and always remembered exactly how much it was and expected more in return. He said he didn't suffer fools gladly. He never suffered anyone gladly, certainly not me." Amazingly, she said this in a monotone — no weeping, no calling of names, no stamping of feet or clutching of fists.

The church seemed to become even longer, darker, and filled now with high school students who sat in class groups. The pastor stood but the place was so poorly lit and the pastor was so far away that he seemed to have no eyes or nose, only a mouth.

He said, "Family and acquaintances have reviewed final Robert. Everyone has spoken who requested the privilege. No one objected that any report has been unfair. Although we held a place on this podium for any who'd speak in his favor, none has come. No vote will be taken today. This isn't an election. We'll bring instead a verdict, unanimous from our human perspective; but it will be announced tomorrow morning.

"Follow along with me through this summary: The final Robert had all the opportunities that everyone else receives. He was surrounded by friends, nurtured by family, taught in the church. Memos on file at the high school state that at several yearly reviews sensitivity training was strongly urged upon him but he refused these suggestions.

"For being what most people considered a respectable person, the final Robert became nearly less than human. He descended about as far as he could go. Therefore, would you all please rise to confirm this sad event."

As one, the gigantic congregation rose as though they were soldiers. They bowed their heads in silence. The pastor spoke in a sad, slow manner: "We have no alternative left but to commit him to the depths."

Robert rolled over in bed against Gladys. In her sleep she pushed him away. Even though the house on this Christmas Eve was chilly, Robert lay on top of the blankets, covered with sweat. He opened, then closed his eyes tightly. All he could think to do was to pray.

Proper 15 / Pentecost 12 / Ordinary Time 20
John 6:51-58
by C. David McKirachan

Such a Deal!

There's this restaurant I frequent in Seabright called the Waterfront Cafe. It's built out on a pier, surrounded by boats. The sunsets are to die for. They have two chefs who can do things with shrimp that are right up there with the sunsets. Marty, the owner, sits at the end of the bar presiding over his domain with a baseball-hat crown. He used to carry around a cigar, until they made it illegal. He comes to church, then goes back to the restaurant and discusses my sermons. It's become a real focus of evangelism. When I go to this place, I'm known, appreciated, and very well fed.

The other day someone asked me if the dinner we get there is worth the price. The question bothered me — it made no sense to me. I tried to answer by saying that the food is exceptional and the service is great, but in the middle of my answer I realized that the value of the place for me has little to do with the price of the meal. I realized that the Waterfront isn't just where I go to buy food. It's full of memories and moments, of relationships and small traditions. I felt like the questioner and I were having two different conversations. To answer him, I'd either have to deny my experience of value to talk in his language of dollars and cents and comparisons with the beer joint down the road, or I'd have to speak in terms that transcended his frame of reference.

Sometimes I wonder why Jesus didn't just fry the idiots that surrounded him. John's gospel is full of these multi-level conversations with truth and glory coming out of the Lord's mouth, with everybody else not getting, not seeing, not even breathing in the same dimension as the Incarnate Word standing before them.

It gets frightening when I use a little humility and realize that I would have probably been one of the idiots. It's easy not to understand. It's easy not to see. It's hard not to keep operating on automatic and to notice that something exceptional is happening right before our eyes. Food's food, money's money, my kid's a pain in the neck, and my schedule is stupid. But here and now we are alive. Here and now eternity intersects our day with a touch and a whisper. Here and now we have an opportunity to taste and see that the Lord is good.

Such multi-dimensional gobbledygook led the Pharisees to mumble and grumble and ask stupid questions like "How can we consume this man's flesh?" I would have fried 'em. But we shouldn't be too hard on them. We have phrases like "measurable and attainable." We choose efficiency over beauty. We teach kids to bisect a cone rather than teaching them how to be intimate or deal with conflict. Yep, I think I'd fry us too.

But he didn't — and he goes on refraining from doing so. He goes on nourishing us in spite of our tendency to worry about the bottom line and to look at our watches when the sermon gets too long. He's more than calories on the hoof for mind, body, and spirit. He's the entree in a banquet of love… and he's the host… and he's the entertainment.

Are we getting our money's worth? If you gotta ask, you can't afford it.

Proper 16 / Pentecost 13 / Ordinary Time 21
1 Kings 8:(1, 6, 10-11) 22-30, 41-43
by David O. Bales

Solomon's Prayer

There were fifteen years of spaghetti suppers and charity golf tournaments. There were fifteen years of scrimping on the present to pay for the future. Some years were stronger than others, with church members whipping up support for the building fund and keeping the goal alive. At other times the project languished, needing another person or group to grab the vision and pull the congregation along. The congregation did it, not the pastors. The decade and a half of saving for the down payment overlapped three pastoral terms. Pastors came and went but the project held together the congregation.

Only one pastor made much of a contribution to the plans. As ideas for the building itself were being garnered during a third capital funds drive, her middle school class was studying First Kings. From that study the group suggested to the long-range planning committee that a Bible quote be painted in the large entryway above the doors. No one had thought of such a thing and when the middle school class suggested a text from Solomon's Prayer for the Dedication of the Temple, people agreed. Few people read the First Kings passage; besides, the building was yet a long ways in the future. Their text, with a few words omitted and then the periods signifying the ellipses also omitted, was to be painted ten feet high around the entryway, so you had to spin to read the whole thing: "When a foreigner, who is not of your people, comes and prays toward this house, then hear in heaven, and do according to all that the foreigner calls to you, so that all the peoples of the earth may know your name and fear you" (1 Kings 8:41-43).

By the time the denomination finally granted a loan for the second two-thirds of the total price, everyone's ideas had been pooled into the building design (including the quote from First Kings, saved dutifully by three high school students) — and the joy of the first shovel turned! Within eight months the congregation moved from their small downtown building, which lacked a parking lot and had too many steps, to their two-acre, one-story campus in the suburbs.

Nineteen months later a group of Hispanic Christians inquired of each congregation in town, requesting a space to rent for worship on Sunday evenings, and maybe a few other evenings too.

The board received the delegation, listening politely and asking a few questions, and would have refused them kindly — if the group hadn't gotten mixed up by the directions the pastor had given over the phone about where to find the board meeting. They came into the building through the main entrance, and they were overjoyed to read, and report to the board that they'd read, what they assumed was the congregation's mission statement in the large entryway: "When a foreigner, who is not of your people, comes and prays toward this house, then hear in heaven, and do according to all that the foreigner calls to you, so that all the peoples of the earth may know your name and fear you."

When the group had departed with many thank-yous, the first and principal reason discussed for not renting the church to them was that "sometimes we need the sanctuary on Sunday evenings."

"When?" asked the pastor, who was one year from retirement.

"Sometimes," the board agreed.

"When was the last time? Have we held any Sunday evening events in the sanctuary since we moved into this building?"

No one could remember any. At that juncture someone moved to table the discussion until the next month's meeting, stating the need for prayer over such a matter.

The word zipped quickly through the membership and few were positive about another group using their church. Three high school students, however, thought it was what the church was for.

Some members might have prayed about it but the high school students didn't see much evidence of prayer. The students did, however, quote the Bible text in the entryway a number of times, having memorized its abbreviated form. During prayer concerns one Sunday, Drusilla, a high school senior, held the microphone with shaking hands and said, "We need to pray about the Hispanic congregation getting a place to worship." Josh on one side of her and Sarah on the other nodded and said, "Yes!"

After worship the three talked to a board member who said, "I guess we could do it — if we had proper guarantees, liability insurance, and all."

When they cornered another board member, she said, "Yes, I've been thinking about it. We all have."

No one in the congregation had been a member of a church that rented its space to another congregation, but one couple had been members of a new congregation that had rented space in a school gym until they'd built a church. The discussion was hot at times. Some people changed their thinking, then changed it back, as ideas both for and against renting passed through the congregation.

Finally, after the issue was tabled two months in a row, the board announced it would vote at Thursday's meeting. The motion to rent, with proper guarantees, liability insurance, and all, was made by a member who first quoted Solomon's prayer as it circled their entryway. Another board member said, "Spare the lecture. Let's vote." The board's decision was...

* * * * *

What do you think? [Raise your hand if you think they voted yes. How many of you think they voted no?] When Jesus told such stories he often ended with something like "Go and do likewise." How would you vote, believing as did Solomon when he prayed for the temple: "Even heaven and the highest heaven cannot contain you, much less this house that I have built!"

Proper 17 / Pentecost 14 / Ordinary Time 22
Mark 7:1-8, 14-15, 21-23
by Larry Winebrenner

Curing Defilement

When the Pharisees washed before eating, they were not trying to destroy germs. The cause of disease had not yet been discovered. It was generally believed that devils caused just about every kind of illness — physical and emotional. Thus the cleansing was not a physical cleansing, but a spiritual one.

I sometimes suspected my grandmother of being a closet Pharisee. You'd better never come to the table with unwashed hands. And among her favorite sayings was "Cleanliness is next to godliness."

Of course, we wash our hands these days for physical cleansing, and rightly so. You would think that the human race would have discovered the importance of clean hands before the middle of the nineteenth century. Not so.

As late as 1870, about half of the people operated on died from infection. It wasn't simply disease filtering in from some other sick person. The infections were caused by the medical staffs themselves. Not only did doctors not wear rubber gloves (they weren't invented yet), they didn't even wash their hands between operations. Doctors wore no smocks or covering, no masks, no protective clothing at all. They did not sterilize instruments. They did not operate in a sterile environment. And when Dr. Joseph Lister proposed these sterile procedures, the medical profession scorned him. They rejected his advice. Only Louis Pasteur was sympathetic.

One of the major reasons for surgery were compound fractures — breaks in which the broken bone penetrates the skin. Infections from compound fractures were so common that doctors would amputate a limb rather than trying to repair the break. Even so, the death rate from amputation infections was 40%. Because of Dr. Lister's work, by 1910 deaths had dropped to 3%.

Dr. Lister revealed great information about the health of our physical bodies. Many modern psychologists believe they have done the same thing for behavior problems. The Great Physician was way ahead of them. Freudians, for example, track emotional problems to the id — a primitive inner self over which we exercise little control. Jesus called it "the heart." All that bad stuff that pops out of you — fornication, theft, murder, adultery, avarice, wickedness, deceit, licentiousness, envy, slander, pride, folly — comes from the heart.

Jesus' point, though, was that you do have control of your heart. Just as one might wash hands, so must one cleanse the heart. Tradition is just fine but obedience is really the important thing.

Proper 18 / Pentecost 15 / Ordinary Time 23
Mark 7:24-37
by C. David McKirachan

Harry Potter Lives

When I was younger I wanted to open a school for Christian wizards. I figured there were a lot of things we should be doing and investigating that we weren't because we were too busy being pastors and preachers and teachers and church runners. I didn't think all the things Jesus did were unique to him and those immediately around him. A lot of his teaching pointed toward the power "at work within us." This wasn't about spells and incantations; it was about unleashing the power of the Holy Spirit to the world. It was about allowing us to be something other than frightened and timid. It was about standing up and saying to demons, "Be gone!" I was young.

After a stint in Newark and then the suburbs and finally as a single parent (I'm not sure which was more difficult), my worldview started to morph. I began to realize that Jesus did not see this miracle-doing as much of an important thing. I began to see that an awful lot of the miracle stuff had to do with the individual to whom it happened. I began to realize that just like anything else we do, it is limited and will pass into dust one day. Our job is to point to the eternal.

I like Harry Potter. He's a confused kid with a lot of hang-ups. Not much of what he does is for any good reason except that it seems to make sense at that particular moment. And the magic part is not much help — it tends to get him into as much trouble as it gets him out of. It's just like any other gift of the spirit. It's very definitely up to you what you're going to get done with the gifts and the opportunities God gives you.

So I have my hole. There are strange things on the walls, and I dabble in magic every time I write a novel. But the powerful magic of my life is much more evident in the classroom and the sanctuary and the hospital room. It's where the spells of teaching and preaching and compassion weave and dance with the music of the Holy Spirit and the souls of those whose hearts and minds are open and receptive. That, my friends, is magic to be sure.

So I guess I am a Christian wizard. I'm glad I don't need a wand — I tend to lose things.

Proper 19 / Pentecost 16 / Ordinary Time 24
Mark 8:27-38
by W. Lamar Massingill

Questions, Answers, and the Difficulties of True Goodness

Questions and answers are always a part of life. Questions begin quests, regardless of whether we find the answers or not. Some questions we just have to, as the German writer Rilke suggests, "continue to live," or live into the answers over a lifetime, and sometimes it takes a lifetime to quest after a question, not to mention answering it.

In our journey this week, we have two questions asked by Jesus: one quite simple, the other simple and simultaneously difficult. Sometimes in a discussion group we have to ask the questioner, "Is that a personal question or an academic one?" Actually, both questions Jesus asked were pretty academic.

All this is to say that some things are right under our noses. So that's why I say both questions were academic and the ones to whom he was asking these were his disciples; people who knew the answers to those questions. It was, however, the way the questions were asked that is the center of our story. The first was certainly academic and the answer would not at all put the disciples in a bind: "Who do people say that I am?" I'm assuming the disciples all jumped on this: well, there are several people we have heard others say you are — John the Baptist, Jeremiah, Elijah, or one of the prophets.

But the second question was the hardest: "Who do *you* say that I am?" It was a hard question because it demanded a commitment on the part of whoever answered the question. It was a hard quest because it demanded that whoever answered it would begin a journey without the knowledge of where that journey would lead them, and the only one that answered it was Peter.

Several years ago, so I'm told, Arthur Miller came to Yale University to give a seminar for college seniors studying his works. The first, of course, was *Death of a Salesman*. "What critics should we read?" the students asked. To which Miller responded, "None. I know what they write. I am interested in what you feel." Must have been scary!

An academic question may be demanding but a personal one on the part of Jesus is consuming and many times dangerous because it pushes one to live the question, always in search of the truth of what it means to follow Jesus: "Who do *you* say that I am?"

So Peter answered the question. And in doing so, Peter had the simultaneous responsibility of having to own and commit himself to this confession. We too will have to take responsibility for our beliefs in time and history. We will have to take the risk of saying "I think," regardless of what others think. We will have to suffer the losses that will accompany our beliefs and also the celebrations that accompany our beliefs. All of this was a part of the question. Jesus forced the issue, not only with Peter but also with all of the disciples. They were not expected simply to listen to the questions and give academic answers. They were expected to live the questions, always in search of the way to follow Jesus. Questions begin quests, remember, and Jesus, through his question, put Peter on a quest that sacred day.

Imagine if Peter had not taken responsibility for his beliefs in Christ. I'm grateful we only have to imagine it. Peter, because he took personal responsibility, gathered the early church into its beginning. And I would be willing to guess that it was this very episode with Jesus that changed him from a spiritual adolescent to a spiritual adult. "Who do you say that I am?" It's an important question for us too — in fact, the question of a lifetime.

No sooner, however, does Peter take the confessional plunge than he finds himself in over his head with his foot in his mouth. His confession wound up — from the text it seems almost immediately — creating a confrontation between Jesus and Peter. It's easy to answer a question, but quite another thing to live both the question and the answers it reveals. That involves pure goodness and we may think it incomprehensible but there is nothing so feared and less confronted than the good in every one of us, because goodness is so demanding yet necessary to follow Jesus in a world such as ours.

"Get thee behind me, Satan!" Jesus says. Well, it's not the friendliest of statements but it is loving. Stop to think about it. It is a deeply loving thing on the part of Jesus not to withhold the hard, plain truth of how Peter was to serve, when that very truth is the only thing that will serve the moment. I say this because I am very suspect of love without confrontation. That's to say, watch out for the sweetness of character that backs off from the pain of confrontation. That's a mushy sentimentality. Love never justifies attitudes that evade reality. So in my vision of this episode, Peter got a good dose of reality. And perhaps in the face and feelings of Peter we would too. Could Jesus be saying the same to us — "Get thee behind me, Satan!" — because of our evasiveness of the difficulties of true goodness?

As if the rebuke of Jesus was not enough, Jesus turns to his disciples to explain the difficulties that the real goodness of discipleship involved: Take up your cross and follow me, deny yourself, whoever shall save his life shall lose it, and whoever loses his life for my sake will save it. For what does it profit a man, to gain the whole world and forfeit his life? All of these describe the difficulty of pure goodness. All of it describes the challenge of a follower of Jesus. And most of these words of Jesus have overtones of withholding from others for ourselves. Clearly Jesus did not believe that better jobs and bigger houses and expensive cars at the expense of generosity to others add up to the abundant life. Peter eventually understood this and along with that lost his evasive repression of reality and put the extra into the ordinary. How did he do it? Because Jesus never ceased to believe in him, and he never ceases to believe in us, regardless of who we are or aren't.

In this context, I suppose a good closing question to take with us on this week's quest is this: To what extent am I willing to risk the courage and responsibility that goes with owning my own images, beliefs, and views about God? Am I willing to liberate my own created goodness? And in doing so, what difference will I make? Think about it.

Proper 20 / Pentecost 17 / Ordinary Time 25
Mark 9:30-37
by John Smylie

Five Days Old

She was only five days old the first time she came to church. She was absolutely tiny — her mom looked incredibly tired and her dad was very, very proud. There were arguments throughout the congregation — some thought the new minister was not traditional enough, others felt the old minister was somewhat of a fuddy-duddy; people argued over the music, they argued over the use of the building. It seemed as if everyone wanted to be in control. The building committee wasn't pleased with the stewardship committee, the stewardship committee was frustrated with the vestry, the vestry was frustrated with the finance committee, the finance committee was frustrated with the congregation and with the stock market... on and on it went. The faith community was clearly frustrated by its own humanness — they were forgetting the glory of God upon which they were founded and upon which their life was based... until a five-day-old little girl came into the church.

Her mother and father had been married for several years and were unable to conceive a child until they came and asked for prayers. They received private prayers and counsel — they were encouraged to let go of their anxieties while enjoying the gifts found in their marriage. And not long after the prayers and counsel, new prayers were offered that the mother who was now pregnant would carry the child to full term. The prayers were heard and the progress was noted as the mother grew and the evidence of their blessing became visible to all. The time came for the child to be born. Mom and Dad kept appearing in church. A few days late... more than a week late... more than two weeks late... and anxiety was rising within some who were particularly close to the couple. Folks were becoming worried about the health of mother and child.

The decision was made that labor would be induced on the Tuesday before that Sunday — and a large and healthy little girl was born, the little girl who would remind us of whom we are and whom we are called to be. She came to church cradled in her father's arms, wrapped in a soft white blanket and barely able to move, and she was the center of everyone's attention. As we looked at her and saw the importance of who she was — the gift of a new life, the miracle of a little girl — we saw hope found within her, and it felt foolish to worry about the things that we were usually worried about. How could we be concerned if the music was traditional or contemporary? We had something to sing about, for joy was in our hearts as we shared in the joy of this young couple and their newborn child. What was so important that we couldn't put our differences aside: the differences between the building committee and the stewardship committee; the differences between the stewardship committee and the vestry; the differences between the vestry and the finance committee; the differences between the finance committee and the congregation? Nothing was more important to us than the sweetness of the little girl who was brought to us on the fifth day of her life.

Babies have a way of bringing healing. Little babies have a way of ministering to us. They don't need to do anything and most of us will realize the grace and ministry of a little child when we feel the warmth of their tiny bodies held against our chests. We are not looking for their opinions; we are not measuring them on their creativity or on their giving of their time or their talents. We don't expect them to do anything but be... be who they are — and even that is met without any expectations. We simply want them to be and to stay warm; we want them to feed and grow. It was the little five-day-old girl who brought us healing and grace and an example of how to be with one another, because on the day she arrived in the congregation we heard the gospel — we really heard the gospel, not just with our ears but with our hearts and with our lives. It was as if Jesus himself was able to penetrate our community with his Word made flesh in the little five-day-old girl as his words were read from the gospel: "Whoever welcomes one such child in my name welcomes me, and whoever welcomes me welcomes not me but the one who sent me."

The gospel — the good news — is around us, within us, and among us.

Proper 21 / Pentecost 18 / Ordinary Time 26
Mark 9:38-50
by John Sumwalt

Whoever Is Not Against Us...

There is a Labor Day event in our community called the St. Marten's Fair. Several thousand people descend on the little village of St. Marten for three days and nights of eating, drinking, and shopping in over a hundred flea-market-like booths lined up on both sides of a mile-long main street. There is live music and some seating but the main activity is walking in a river of people about seven deep on one side and eight or nine deep going the other direction. Some fairgoers push carts crammed with heirloom tomatoes and other fruits and vegetables from the farm markets interspersed along the way. Others are drinking fresh-squeezed lemonade or eating buttered sweet corn, greasy curly fries, and spare ribs dripping with barbecue sauce. All are filled with a festival spirit heightened by the warm sun and a cool breeze on a perfect summer day.

Hawkers who work at computers in cubicles during the week shout out their wares over the din of the crowd. "Ice cold water here, one dollar!" "Try our fresh kettle corn!" "T-shirts, sunglasses, belts for three dollars, today only!"

Zealous religious folks can be seen sitting quietly at their booths behind loud signs that cry out, "Are you going to heaven?" and "Jesus saves!" Mostly they are left alone. People stream by, seemingly avoiding even a glance in their direction. A dejected but determined-looking man sitting in something called a "Godmobile" must be thinking, "Anyone who witnesses for the Lord must expect to be ignored by the world."

There is one booth that advertises "spiritually inspired paintings." They are covered with squiggly, abstract designs painted in a variety of pastel colors. The artist points to one painting, saying, "This is Jesus, the good shepherd, caring for his sheep." She says spiritual phrases can be seen on some of the paintings, legible because of the way the paint has dried.

An interested fairgoer comments that "perhaps this was 'spirit'-guided, something like automatic writing that occurs when a person's hand is directed by some unseen force and results in beautiful poetry or music."

"Oh, no," the artist declares defensively, "this is not automatic writing! It's from the Holy Spirit!" (emphasis on "Holy").

The fairgoer wonders if "spirit" and "Holy Spirit" might be the same thing. The artist becomes more animated in her resistance, insisting that her paintings are Christian and not just inspired by "spirit." The fairgoer doesn't know what to say. He tries to explain that, like her, he is a follower of Jesus, but that in his church there is a belief that "Spirit," by whatever name, is understood to be "Holy" and can be present in any person regardless of religious affiliation. The artist responds angrily at this suggestion and begins to launch into a long-practiced diatribe. The fairgoer turns away quietly and moves on to the next booth.

Proper 22 / Pentecost 19 / Ordinary Time 27
Mark 10:2-16
by David O. Bales

"The Book"

All signs within the congregation indicated that Reverend Canliss had accomplished what he could with his limited abilities and decreasing energy. Over his four decades of ministry he'd learned to understand a congregation and to do what was best for God's people, even at his own expense. The congregation threw a grand retirement party. Many former parishioners and old pastor friends traveled miles to join the celebration. Reverend Canliss was gratified. Molly Canliss was thrilled, as were their two sons and daughter who came in order to enjoy the reunion with family and friends.

However, Reverend Canliss avoided "The Book." It was presented to him in worship and was bound with gracious and grateful letters from members of his congregations and beyond. On the first morning of his retirement, Molly thumbed "The Book" and scanned a few letters: "Arnold wrote one from Midvale."

"Oh," he said, fumbling with the newspaper.

"And the Nelsons. Remember their family and the cabin at the lake?"

"Un-huh," he said.

Molly realized he didn't want to read "The Book" at that time and she said no more. She placed it on his chest of drawers in the bedroom and there it remained for half a year. After six months Reverend Canliss had finished the projects he'd planned for retirement, yet he still hadn't read "The Book." It sat on the chest of drawers with all the attraction to him of a legal summons.

He'd never sought the limelight, and he'd realized years before that while pastors take much criticism they don't deserve, many people also heap praise upon them that they haven't earned. One morning Molly saw him staring at "The Book" and said, "I know it's hard, but you owe it to the people who wrote the letters." She touched his arm, then abandoned him to his thoughts. He remained standing and staring for another minute. Then the Reverend Canliss, Honorably Retired, grabbed the volume and left the house. He drove to the library, planning to read it in one sitting in order to do his duty: Read "The Book" and clear his conscience.

After two hours reading, the following letter occurred:

Dear Reverend Canliss,

I hope you remember me. If you don't, that's okay. I'm comfortable just knowing that you'll read this. I was in your first congregation in Charlotte. You were right out of seminary. My memory is fuzzy, but I think you and Molly had come to our congregation about eighteen months before I talked with you about the matter for which I am writing you now.

I was on the board and I was most irritated by you. We'd welcomed you with open arms, but you had seemed to change from a happy to a grumpy person. I'd never liked your sermons. Part of it was because they were different from any I'd heard before, but also because it seemed that all you'd do on Sunday was quote a scripture, say a few sentences about it, and then quote another. To me they never seemed very connected.

I've reflected upon our relationship. I understand now that my irritation with you was multiplied by the anguish I was experiencing in my own life. My wife and I weren't happy; yet it seemed that as Sundays went by, I became more miserable and your sermons became more rigid and unloving.

I was trying to be a faithful Christian and loyal to the church, but my home life poisoned everything I touched — including my faith, the church, and my opinion of you. After mentioning to you a few times (in indirect ways) that your sermons offered little help in getting the Bible into the modern world, I made up my mind to get you alone and put this question straight to you. I picked the circumstances carefully so we'd have time and so you couldn't get away. I asked you: "Is it lawful for a man to divorce his wife?"

You stood quiet for a long while, and then you spoke slowly, saying something like, "Yes, it is lawful. But it will cost you a lifetime of pain and regret and you'll miss the blessings God has planned for you with your wife and family."

I expected you to reel off some scriptures but you answered me clearly, succinctly, and in a reasoned way. I was dumbfounded — and thoroughly answered. From then on I found what you said in your sermons to be much more merciful and practical. I realized you had a great deal to say about how to struggle with the problems that all Christians face.

I don't think I thanked you then or later, but I do now. I can look at our three children and our grandchildren. They would never have existed if it weren't for your advice. I can honestly assess my relationship with my wife and promise you that it became better — although slowly. I won't say any more. Please believe me that my wife and our family enjoyed the (at times difficult) blessings that God planned for us. She died three years ago May.

This is my belated thank you and my prayer for God's blessings upon you.

The letter had no signature. The Reverend Robert Canliss, Honorably Retired, carefully breathed in and out, not wanting to make a spectacle of himself in the public library. He remembered with cinematic clarity that afternoon forty years before when Monty Anderson stepped into his office and asked him point-blank the question he himself had been struggling with in his own marriage. Once more he recalled that turning point in his life when it was necessary for the sake of his congregation to do more than quote scripture, and to share what he'd only recently come to realize about his own marriage problems.

Proper 23 / Pentecost 20 / Ordinary Time 28
Mark 10:17-31
by C. David McKirachan

Desperation's Opportunity

Just before I started my last year of seminary, we had a sit-down with somebody from the Committee on Preparation for Ministry. They said, "Don't expect to get a job right out of seminary." It seemed there was a glut of pastors at the moment and we had to wait for a few of them to retire or surrender before we could get our feet in the door.

I wanted to preach but green people (I don't mean tree-huggers) weren't high on the list of candidates for jobs. So a year later I was pumping gas and working in a leather factory and sending out resumés.

I finally got an interview. It was at a little church on the border of Newark. A few years previously there had been a machine-gun emplacement in the front yard during the riots. The neighborhood wasn't very scenic. The salary was infinitesimal. There were issues with just about every arena of church life. This was a battle zone of a parish. It was inner-city and becoming brutal. I never would have looked at it — I knew what I wanted to do; I knew what my gifts were. This was not the dirt I wanted to be planted in.

But there's an old saying: "Any port in a storm." I was laboring with gale-force winds and swells that were coming over the rails. My parents were patient and kind, but I was getting desperate for a job. I wanted to be ordained — after all, I'd been called. Why hadn't I been chosen?

Taking all of the above into account, I went for the job, got it, and began my ministry. A lot of things got done there in five years. One of those things was that I found out it wasn't my ministry… it was the Lord's. All the strategies and goals I had locked in, all the skills and talents I was so sure of, all the agendas and accomplishments I had planned and focused on became yesterday's fantasies in the face of the city's onslaught. These people didn't need my plans, they needed God's presence. To get to that truth, I had to let go of a lot of stuff. It wasn't fun; it was scary as hell. But it was what I had to do to be a pastor, there or anywhere.

Desperation isn't very sexy. But it is very good at stripping away our illusions and our pride — and we are more likely to humbly grasp the hand that is offered. The hand may be scarred and even bleeding… but it is a hand that offers the incredible gift of partnership in a ministry of compassion, of being a light in the darkness that too often we're busy avoiding.

Proper 24 / Pentecost 21 / Ordinary Time 29
Mark 10:35-45
by Peter Andrew Smith

Achieving Greatness

"So what do you think?" Paul asked as he gestured at the office. "The finest oak desk, state-of-the-art computers, and not one but two personal secretaries."

"Fancier than my corner office, for sure," Sarah said. "And?"

"And?" Paul said. "Explain to me why someone else was recognized for his Christian service in the community. This company is a huge employer and I am the one running it."

"It's not about the bottom line," Sarah said. "You know that."

"I know it isn't." Paul waved for her to sit in a leather chair. "But Tom Bernard? I had to make some calls to even find out who he is. He's a mid-level manager with a small company. What could he possibly contribute to the community that I don't? My company alone donates more in a month than his company did all year."

"You still don't get it, do you?"

"Get it?" Paul said. "Of course I get it. The whole thing must be a popularity contest."

Sarah rolled her eyes. "Paul, how long have we known each other?"

"Since grade school. You're one of my oldest friends."

"Do you trust my opinion?"

"Of course I do. You and Jean-Marc are the godparents to my girls. Tanya and I asked you because we know you are both good Christians."

"Then listen to me. Tom was recognized by the Christian Service Association because he was the best person. The vote for him was unanimous."

"But I thought you were on the selection committee."

"I am. I voted for Tom."

Paul sat up in his chair. "How could you do that when you know the great work I did getting that school built in Africa? Who did you come to when you needed money raised for disaster relief or for that expansion to the church? Didn't I come through?"

"Paul, you work miracles in getting people to give. All those projects were an overwhelming success. You know that."

"Then how could you, my best friend, think that Tom Bernard deserved the award over me?"

Sarah got up from her chair. "Can you take lunch now?"

"I'm not really hungry."

"Then don't eat. I need to show you something."

Paul spoke to one of his secretaries for a moment and then followed Sarah down the stairs.

"Where are we going?" he asked as they started walking away from the bustling office district into an older area of town with fading paint and cracked sidewalks.

"The outreach mission," Sarah said.

Paul stopped. "I've seen the place. Remember, I was on the board of directors a couple of years ago."

"Ever been inside?"

"Lots of times. I was the one who argued with the contractor about the roof."

Sarah sighed. "Ever been inside at this time of day?"

Paul shrugged and trailed behind her to the familiar sight of the outreach mission. The main room of the mission was a beehive of activity as hungry people were served a hot meal.

"Whatever they are cooking smells good," Paul said.

Sarah smiled. "I figured your stomach would win over your hurt feelings. Grab a seat."

"I wouldn't want to take food from someone who needs it..."

"There is always plenty of spaghetti," Sarah said. She waved at the person closest to the kitchen and held up two fingers. "Besides, the volunteers are always happy when local businesspeople drop by and see how things are going."

Steaming plates of spaghetti and cups of coffee soon appeared at their table.

"Mind if I join you, Sarah?" the server asked.

"Please," Sarah said. "Paul Johnson, this is Tom Bernard."

"A pleasure to meet you," Tom said as he shook Paul's hand. "You're a bit of a legend around here for getting the contractor not only to fix the roof but replacing those leaky windows."

"Thanks," Paul said. "Are you on the board of directors here at the outreach mission?"

"No, I'm just a volunteer."

They made small talk as they ate the hearty meal. A scruffy man in a tattered coat standing off to one side gestured for Tom, and he excused himself from the table.

"Well?" Sarah said.

"Okay. He is a nice fellow," Paul said. "And he certainly does know everyone."

"He should. He helps out here every lunch hour."

"Wow," Paul sipped at his coffee. "That is dedication."

"That's not the half of it. When we started asking around we found out he has been here at every lunch hour for the last five years."

"Five years?" Paul looked at Tom carrying dishes toward the kitchen. "Really?"

"Every day from eleven to one he helps out. When there aren't enough volunteers he comes back after work to wash dishes." Sarah finished the last of her spaghetti. "That's why we chose to recognize his service."

"I think you made the right choice." Paul closed his eyes for a moment, and when he opened them he looked at his watch. "You in a rush to get back to the office?"

"Why?"

"I'm free for another half-hour, and I can imagine there are lots of dirty dishes piling up in the kitchen. Do you suppose Tom could use some help cleaning up?"

Sarah smiled, and two more servants of Christ began to clear away the tables.

Proper 25 / Pentecost 22 / Ordinary Time 30
Job 42:1-6, 10-17; Hebrews 7:23-26
by Argile Smith

Mistaken Identity

Maggie had just plopped into her favorite recliner when her phone rang. She didn't really want to answer it. The day had drained her energy. At work she seemed to be running into one problem after another. The people she supervised had behaved as if she had insulted them simply because she tried to supervise them. Not interested in her input, they didn't appear to be interested in working either. Only one activity interested them: whining. All of their energies that day had been invested in complaining, griping, and throwing pity parties. She could hardly wait to get away from them at the end of the day.

When she got home, she wondered if she had somehow taken a wrong turn and had gone right back to work. Her two teenage daughters let her know immediately upon crossing the threshold into her house that they didn't want her telling them what to do. They complained that she had been overbearing and that she never allowed them to spend time with their friends.

Their complaints spewed from them like lava from an active volcano. The seismic activity in their souls had been activated by her edict a couple of days earlier. That's when she grounded both of them because they had brought home some terrible grades at school. And that's when their anger at her began to boil.

She held her tongue through dinner. As she listened to them grumble about the food, the apartment, the restrictions placed on them, and the way that life made no sense any more, she wanted to snarl at them about responsibility and appreciating when their mother tried to provide for them. Instead, she remained silent in the awareness that talking wouldn't do any good at that moment. She knew that her words would turn into weapons-grade verbal blasts. She couldn't forgive herself if she wounded her daughters' souls with harsh, cruel words. So she kept quiet.

After dinner, everyone left for their own space. Her daughters went to their bedroom to grieve their confinement and to refine their strategies to make their mom's life miserable. Maggie went to the living room, fell into her easy chair, and turned on the television to escape the difficulties of the day, and to unwind a little before going to bed.

So her decision about answering her phone didn't come easily. She decided to answer the call when she noticed that the caller's number looked, well, curious. She recognized the area code but the number didn't seem to register with her. So she said to herself, "What's it going to hurt to answer the call? My day's already been shot. This call can't make it any worse."

But in a way, it did. The guy on the other end of the line claimed to be the president of the university from which she had graduated. He called because he wanted to keep in touch with alumni like her.

Of course, Maggie didn't buy his claim. Why would the president of her university be calling her anyway? She had graduated years earlier and she hadn't made a contribution to the alumni fund. Besides, she recalled that the president of her university had retired a couple of years earlier. She reasoned that the guy on the other end of the line must be either a prankster or a sales representative. Either way she wasn't interested, so she hung up on him in mid-sentence.

He called her back right away. Mad about her day and frustrated with her kids, she reacted to the call by answering it — but not to listen to the caller's pitch. She used it as an opportunity to ventilate. As soon as he started talking, she unloaded her entire arsenal of verbal weaponry on him, letting him have it for every offense from interrupting her evening to occupying space on the planet. Then she hung up again, this time with a little more satisfaction. She had used the faceless voice as a punching bag. Now she felt better. Soon she drifted off to sleep in her easy chair.

Three days later she got a personal note in the mail from the university. Her address had been written by hand on the envelope, and the words "President's Office" had been embossed on the card inside. The note simply read: "Sorry about offending you with my phone call. I'm new at this work, and I'm trying to find ways to get feedback from our alumni. Every night I call five alums at random. That's why you got the call. Again, sorry I bothered you."

Job didn't have a clear picture of the Lord when he complained in his misery. Clarity came when the Lord confronted him (Job 42:1-6, 10-17). Likewise, some of the Hebrew Christians had lost sight of Jesus Christ and his place in their lives. For that reason, the pastor of the congregation tried to help them to sharpen their perspective on Jesus Christ (Hebrews 7:23-28). The Lord wants to bless us and we don't want to miss the blessing of an intimate relationship with him because of mistaken identity.

Reformation
Jeremiah 31:31-34
by C. David McKirachan

People with Chests

Freud came up with the Oreo cookie theory of the personality. Good theory... but he copied the biblical idea. They saw the head as analytical, the gut as passion, and the heart as the place of decision and commitment. It's the place of loyalty and courage. That makes a lot more sense than our cute-ifying of the heart. It's nice for Hallmark moments — but when it comes to standing up in the face of difficulty, hearts and flowers don't have a prayer. C.S. Lewis said, "What we need are people with chests."

As a kid, I watched my parents standing in the face of trouble. Dad was the pastor of a large church in a lily-white community that wanted to stay that way. He stood up for integration and this delightful upper-class bunch of people grew fangs. We heard a lot of back and forth about how a minister shouldn't get involved in social issues. He didn't back down. Then it got uglier.

We lived on a nice quiet street. We had a nice picture window that looked out on our front lawn, shaded by maples and oaks. We were watching TV one evening when the peace was literally shattered. A softball-sized rock blew through the big window, sending chunks of glass flying all over the room. My father was on his feet and out the door to watch a car squealing down the street. He came back in and we took inventory. No cuts, just a case of the shakes. My mother picked up the rock and undid the rubber band holding a note. My mother was five feet tall, but as I watched her stand there reading the missive that had been sent to scare us, I stopped shaking. She smiled and said, "At least they told the truth and spelled everything correctly." She handed it to me. In crude language, it informed us that we loved a whole race of people. They thought it was an insult. My father took the note. He turned to me and said, "Blessed are those who are persecuted for righteousness' sake." They blew my mind.

The next morning we found out our buddies had slashed our tires. My father replaced the window. Nobody offered to pay for it or the tires. I got beat up a few times at school. They called me what had been written on the note. When I said, "Yeah, I do. Why don't you?" they didn't like it.

I guess a bit of that heart business rubbed off on me. I hope so — my parents were people with chests. That's another word for heroes.

All Saints
Revelation 21:1-6
by C. David McKirachan

Strut Your Stuff

One of my favorite things about being a minister is marrying people. There are few more highly motivated human beings on the planet than brides. Most grooms are confused and nervous. But something happens to a woman when she puts on a wedding dress. The risk and sorrow and trouble and stress of life and marriage melt away like sugar in a flood. What is left is a vision that somehow the bride inhales. For a few moments the difficulties of life, the disappointments and vicissitudes, all take a backseat and are silenced by that vision of glory that is being a bride.

Others in the bridal party are not gifted with this vision. They usually need a little work. During the rehearsal, I tell those preceding the one in white that everyone will be looking at them as they walk down the aisle. If they choose to attempt to seem small, curling in on themselves, everyone will be looking at them as they attempt to hide in plain sight. The only option at this point is to strut their stuff. I tell them, "Realize you are the most gorgeous example of you on the planet and that the bride has chosen you to accompany her in her glory. Wow 'em." Many of them giggle. Some of them look at me like a pain. Some of them planned to do that anyway.

As the Body of Christ, too often we curl in on ourselves because we are embarrassed, because we've been taught that we shouldn't be showy or stand out or be rude. We mistake self-confidence for arrogance. But each of us is the best example of us that is on the planet and we have been invited by the Lord to accompany him in his journey from glory into glory. Where do we get off trying to hide behind a lousy body image or excuses about how lavender just isn't our color? We need to get over our paltry excuses. This is our opportunity to strut our stuff, to be saints, to be examples of Christ's glory that set the stage for his coming.

Besides, the reception is coming — and that's going to be a blast.

Proper 26 / Pentecost 23 / Ordinary Time 31
Mark 12:28-34
by Larry Winebrenner

The Scribe

Benjamin thought back to the days when he received his training as a scribe.

"Everyone can read," said the rabbi. "Only the scribe can write."

He smiled at the thought of the rabbi fibbing. Everyone could not read. There were women... and beggars... and even businessmen who grew up in other nations.

Nor were only scribes able to write. Sure, wealthy businessmen hired scribes to scribble for them. But it was not uncommon for a man to write identifying names on bundles of merchandise.

However, Benjamin knew what the rabbi meant. Only a scribe was trained in the law sufficiently to write without unintentionally blaspheming the Lord. There were 631 laws one had to be careful not to break. He thought about that. How many times had he and his colleagues discussed — no, argued about — which of these laws were most important?

A favorite approach was to say, "Suppose you were in a situation where obeying one law meant breaking another, and not to obey in order to avoid breaking the other law meant you were breaking by not obeying?" The arguments often got very convoluted. They also got very silly. "Say a swarm of hornets was about to attack a man. You can thwart their attack by lighting a smudge pot so the man can stand in the smoke. If you don't do this, it is tantamount to murder. But if it is the sabbath, do you avoid being a murderer by breaking another law and do sabbath work by lighting the smudge pot?" Silly and confusing.

Enough of this daydreaming. It was a beautiful day. Walking in the groves cleared his head. It actually inspired him. Hadn't the psalmist written, "The Lord made heaven and earth, the sea, and all that is in them"?

When he considered the heavens in their starry glory and singing birds, when he examined the earth filled with green growth, the animals, and all creation, his voice exploded with the psalmist's words: "Bless the Lord, O my soul!"

Some of the younger scribes and Pharisees laughed when they heard his reedy voice holding forth. He was no great singer, but he was a great praiser — and a great scribe. He knew the scriptures by heart. He was ready to be called rabbi when he celebrated his fortieth birthday in a few weeks. Let the young pretenders laugh… some of them would never make the grade.

His walk eventually took him into the marketplace. Sometimes it was refreshing to listen to public debates among the young scribes. It gave him an opportunity to enlighten the more facile minds. It was one of his favorite activities. As often happened when he entered the marketplace, one such debate was under way. Instead of the scribes arguing among themselves, they had ganged up on a traveling preacher.

Benjamin had heard of the preacher — Yeshua, or in that barbaric Greek tongue, Jesus. Thank goodness the man spoke Aramaic instead of the harsh Greek language. Yeshua had a reputation for knowing the scriptures as well as a fully trained scribe, so Benjamin listened to the debate with interest.

Like so many of the young scribes still trying to make a name for themselves, they were resorting to the tired old arguments so common they were boring. Yeshua seemed to be enjoying himself. Someone would ask him one of these commonplace arguments. Instead of the traditional response, Yeshua would introduce a telling scripture reference from a totally unexpected context.

"To obey is better than sacrifice," intoned one young scribe, lifting up King Saul's refusal to obey God's command to destroy everything, even the cattle in his battle against the Amalekites. "Does that mean sacrifices are of no value?"

Yeshua smiled, almost laughed. "What if sacrifice is not at issue," he responded, "like that pillar of salt on Mount Sodom?"

They had to ponder a moment. This seemed so out of context to their argument. Benjamin chuckled to himself. This Yeshua was a bright young man.

Before long the scribes realized Yeshua was referring to Lot's wife. She was turned into a pillar of salt for disobedience. Benjamin decided it was time for a lesson. He walked up to the group. They parted like the Red Sea of old and smugly allowed him to pass. This scribe about to become a rabbi would put this thorn in his place.

Benjamin came face-to-face with Yeshua. "Which commandment is the first of all the commandments?"

Yeshua looked deeply into Benjamin's eyes. Benjamin felt his soul being examined. Without humor, Yeshua answered the question. It was not an argument. It was a straightforward answer to a serious question. "The first is 'Hear, O Israel: the Lord our God, the Lord is one; you shall love the Lord your God with all your heart, and with all your soul, and with all your mind, and with all your strength.' "

Yeshua paused just a moment, just long enough for a response if there were to be one. Benjamin looked deeply into Yeshua's eyes, waiting for more. Yeshua didn't disappoint him.

"The second is this," he continued. " 'You shall love your neighbor as yourself.' There is no other commandment greater than these."

Benjamin gave a slight nod. He addressed Yeshua with a term of respect, but he spoke to the young scribes. "You are right, Teacher; you have truly said that 'he is one, and besides him there is no other'; and 'to love him with all the heart, and with all the understanding, and with all the strength,' and 'to love one's neighbor as oneself' — this is much more important than all whole burnt offerings and sacrifices."

Yeshua smiled. The words he said to Benjamin were burned into the scribe's soul. "You are not far from the kingdom of God."

The young scribes looked from Benjamin to Yeshua and back again. They wandered off, leaving the two men standing there. But they never again engaged Yeshua in debate.

Proper 27 / Pentecost 24 / Ordinary Time 32
Mark 12:38-44
by John Sumwalt

Giving All

Gerald Fitzgerald was the biggest giver at First Redeemer Church. Fitz, as he was called, was the owner of his own business and well-known for his generosity. Because of this, he had often been called on by the leaders in the congregation to head up the annual pledge drive. One year, while going over the pledges from the previous year, Fitz was surprised to discover that the second biggest pledge in the church was almost as much as his pledge. Fitz didn't recognize the name of the pledger, so when it was time to assign the callers for visitation Sunday, he added Midge Griswold's name to the list of people that he would personally call on.

Fitz was curious about who Midge was. No one on his committee had recognized her name. The pastor said she was a new member who had joined the congregation the year before. Fitz looked forward to meeting Midge. He thought she must be quite a wealthy woman if she was able to give almost as much he did. Perhaps she was an older woman who had inherited money from her husband or her family. She must live in a grand house in a nice neighborhood. Maybe he and his wife could invite her over for dinner sometime. If she was new in the church, she might welcome an opportunity to meet some of the congregation's leaders.

When Fitz pulled up in front of a small apartment building, which according to his directions was where Midge lived, he checked the address twice to make sure he was at the right place. She must own the building, Fitz thought to himself. He told the young woman who answered the door of the very modest apartment that he was looking for Mrs. Griswold. "I'm Midge Griswold," the young woman replied. "What can I do for you?" Fitz was so taken aback that he almost forgot why he had come. Finally he managed to tell her that he was from the church and he had come to pick up her pledge for the next year. "Oh, of course," Midge said, "I've been expecting you. Come and sit down while I fill it out."

Fitz noticed a picture of an older couple on the end table and he asked Midge who they were. "They are my grandparents," Midge said. "They are missionaries in Haiti. That's where I grew up. Grandpa and Grandma raised me after my folks died." Midge handed Fitz her pledge card. She hadn't bothered to put it in an envelope, so Fitz couldn't help but see that Midge's pledge for the next year was substantial. Indeed, it was considerably more than his own. Fitz couldn't help himself. He was startled. How could such a young woman with apparently modest means afford to give so much? Fitz wasn't ordinarily a nosy person, but in this instance he couldn't help himself; he had to know.

"Miss Griswold," Fitz began in a more formal voice than he intended, "I am curious about your pledge." Immediately a look of great concern came over Midge's face, and before Fitz could go on to explain himself she interrupted him and said, "I hope it's enough. I know I'm not giving as much as I should. Nurses make good money here but the cost of living is so much higher than it is in Haiti. I can't seem to give any more than a tithe. I'm hoping to do better next year. The need in the world is so great and our church does so much good. I want to help all I can."

"Oh, don't worry," Fitz said. "You're doing just fine. We are very fortunate to have you as a part of our congregation."

With that, Fitz bid Midge a hasty good-bye and left as quickly as he could. He was deeply troubled by Midge's generosity. How can she live like that, Fitz wondered? Giving so much — it's not practical. But what troubled him most was how much he was going to have to raise his own pledge.

Proper 28 / Pentecost 25 / Ordinary Time 33
Mark 13:1-8
by Peter Andrew Smith

A Stronger Foundation

There once was a young man who was clever and strong. In school he received top marks, and on the athletic field he was a star player. He had many admirers and friends who surrounded him wherever he went. Everyone who knew him believed that he had everything he needed to succeed in life. Yet the young man thought there must be something more than school and sports.

The young man graduated and went to university on a full scholarship. He was popular on campus and received academic awards and sports trophies. He had plenty of friends and caught the eye of many young women, who admired his popularity and good looks. The young man had everything he wanted in life — yet he still couldn't shake the feeling that he was missing something.

He grew older and when he finished his studies the man was recruited by a thriving company. He quickly made his mark in the business world and leapt up the corporate ladder. He found he didn't have as much time for sports anymore but he still played in recreational leagues. He met a special woman who made his heart sing and made him think about his future. His coworkers considered him the golden boy — but the man still looked for more in his life.

Romance led to marriage and children. The man worked hard to provide for his family and took on extra responsibility to get ahead in his career. He continued to excel in everything he did in the office, at home, and on the sports field. He considered his world and decided he had everything there was to have in life — a rewarding career, a loving wife and children, and a home of his own.

The man continued to work hard and get promotions. With his busy career and his commitment to sports, he found his children growing up without him and his wife becoming a stranger. When he confided his uneasiness to his friends they told him he simply needed to manage his time better. The man tried but he found that even when he was able to find time for family, work, and recreation, the stress of trying to be everything and do everything did not go away.

On the way to work one morning his car slid on a patch of ice and slammed into a concrete barrier. When he woke up in the hospital, the man found that his body had been broken and his confidence shaken by the crash. Everyone around him said his survival was a miracle and a blessing. Faced with a long and difficult recovery and the loss of so much, the man was not so sure.

The man's life changed during the next few years. He was unable to continue in his high-powered position as he recovered from the accident and he found himself in a less demanding role in the company. His body wasn't up to playing sports, so he settled on helping out with his children's teams. His friends and coworkers felt sorry for him but the man became aware that he was discovering something important.

He reconnected with his wife and children. The times they played games together or simply talked continued to be the highlight of his day, even after he returned to work. He was now a part of his children's daily lives and he helped them grow and discover their way in life. The visits from the local pastor when he was in the hospital led him back to church. Time for prayer and Bible reading and Sunday worship became part of his family's life.

When he limped to his car to go home after work, the executives of the company and those who had known him as a star athlete pitied the man. He sometimes thought of his former career and sports days with a tinge of sadness when he drove home. Yet as he pulled into the driveway and was greeted by his children and saw his wife, that feeling was replaced by thankfulness as the man praised God for the way his life had turned out.

Thanksgiving
Matthew 6:25-33
by C. David McKirachan

See?

This chunk of scripture opens two doors for me. One of them brings me to a hill above a banana grove on the eastern bank of the Sea of Galilee. I stood there and saw the hill curving away at my feet like an amphitheater to the right and left. The guide told me that tradition has it that this was the site of the Sermon on the Mount. It makes sense. He could have sat down there in the banana grove, spoken in normal tones, and been heard by everyone on the hill, with 20,000 women and kids. And as he spoke, their view was not only of him, but of the hills that fall away down to the water of the sea. It is a place of green and blooming. "Consider the lilies…" would have been accompanied with a sweep of his hand.

The other door opens onto walks with my mother. She was so close to the earth and sometimes I thought she practiced the old religions by the light of the moon. Anything she touched bloomed with abandon. Anytime we walked anywhere it was an education in seeing, appreciating, and sensing the connections that are there among all things. She knew the Latin names of every weed and flower. She recognized every bird by its song and plumage. But names and categories were only labels. She knew them, saw them, appreciated them, and knew how to share life with them. We invariably came home from our walks with a salad, picked by the wayside.

We live horribly separated lives. We yearn for the touch of love every day. We ache to be known by another, to trust and be appreciated for who we are, not what we do and thus judged by what we don't. But we live in fear and separation as a rule. It is exhausting and debilitating. To pause in our rush of fatigue and stress is almost more than we can manage. Yet this day of Thanksgiving draws us like a magnet even in our brokenness. We want something that just might be here, even if we don't quite know how to find it.

These two humans, the Lord and my mother, shared something very basic, though separated by millennia. Both were connected to the world around them by a deep appreciation for the gift of life and all its diverse glory. They paid attention. They saw. And it made them grateful. Their connection to life made them children of eternity. It's what makes any of us blessed enough to share the gift eternal. And in the face of such wonder and delight, anxiety doesn't have a chance.

On this day of remembrance, I pray that perhaps we might pause long enough to actually notice the gift we've been given; to see; to embrace; to offer a profound "Wow!" to the universe and its maker. Just don't try to eat the weeds unless you know what you've picked.

Christ the King / Proper 29
Revelation 1:4b-8
by David O. Bales

Seeing the End

"At least the preacher wasn't too religious," James said. He pouched out his cheeks as was his older brother manner when speaking the summary of his thoughts.

"And he pronounced 'Smythe' correctly," Dorie said. "Better than that preacher at Aunt Wilma's funeral." She sat at the kitchen table, looking right and left as she spoke to her two brothers. The early evening wind blew hard against the house. Everyone else had left the reception at their father's home. Just the three grown children remained now, without their spouses, in the kitchen of their dead parents' home.

James and Dorie looked at Phil because, by a lifetime of practice, it was now his turn in the rotation to comment on their father's funeral. Dorie tapped her foot under the kitchen table. James remained standing, arms crossed, his back against the refrigerator.

Beside the kitchen window Phil watched the wind strip the last leaves from their parents' giant cherry tree. He was 35 and the youngest. He chewed his gum slowly. His sister and brother waited as they listened to the breeze. Phil was next in the siblings' order to speak.

James, deciding to wait no longer, coughed and offered another observation. "And the music wasn't as bad as I feared." He ended the sentence on an upturn, for Phil to pick up conversation; but Phil furrowed his brow with a deeper look of concentration.

"I think Mom would have liked it," Dorie said, tapping her foot now against the leg of the kitchen table. She turned again to Phil as though handing a baton. But the room fell silent. After two or three minutes James said, "Come on, Phil." He held out his arms toward Phil. "What did you think of Dad's funeral?"

Phil moved a step toward them, although still half turned to the window. The wind pushed a few drops of rain sideways against the glass. He spoke quietly. "Dad kept saying he wanted to see the end of the building project."

James said, "Absolutely. He was fixated on it. Even when I was here a month ago and he'd entered the hospital for the first time, he'd say, 'I want to see the end of it.' "

Their father had taken the chairmanship of the church's fund-raising for a new building. The congregation had raised the money and the construction of the gym and classroom complex was nearly complete.

"I'm just amazed he got into the religion stuff at all," Dorie said. "He never even talked about church when we were kids. I think neighbors took him to church after Mom died."

"Well, they saw his abilities real fast," James said. "They threw him into the chairmanship after only a couple years. 'I've got to see the end of it,' he'd say. Like he was obsessed. I thought maybe in the last month he'd had a little stroke thrown into his heart problems."

Phil said, "I was able to drive and visit him once a week in the last month and a half before he died, and he had graphs and charts and blueprints in the house. He was pretty sincere about it, 'I got it started. I want to see the end of it.' Seems that's all he could think of."

"But the service," Dorie said, bringing them back to the subject at hand.

"It was short enough," James said as he laughed, "even though the preacher wandered from beginning to end. He seemed like the cowboy who jumped on his horse and rode off in all directions."

"Yeah," Dorie said, "but he made such a big deal out of Dad's peace at the end, even when he read from that Revelations book."

"He was trying to make a point, I could tell," James said. "It sailed over me, and I think over everybody. Who reads Revelations at a funeral? Pretty baffling stuff: alpha, omega."

Dorie said, "I think he said that seven times in seven minutes, and each time talking about how calm Dad had been during the last week."

"That he was," James said. "In fact, a couple times when I was with him in the hospital he smiled and cried at the same time. He wasn't upset, I'm sure, even though he couldn't talk well. And like a recording he mentioned the end again. The last thing he mumbled was that he'd seen the end. And he smiled. I guess I hadn't told you two that."

"No," Dorie said, "you hadn't. He smiled? Said he'd seen the end?"

Phil was chewing his gum harder, his brow more wrinkled, nearly a frown. "That Revelation the pastor read." Dorie and James nodded their heads. "The alpha and omega he kept repeating."

"Those are Greek letters," James said. "I wondered when he read it if that's why fraternities got Greek letters."

Phil stopped chewing his gum, "Well, alpha and omega are the beginning and end of the Greek alphabet. And the Bible said that God was the alpha and the omega."

Dorie's foot stopped. Her eyes became very wide. "So God's the beginning," she said as she turned to James, who spoke slowly, "and Dad saw the end."

About the Authors

David O. Bales was a Presbyterian (USA) pastor for 33 years, and is a graduate of the University of Portland (where he was editor of the yearbook) and San Francisco Theological Seminary. In addition to his ministry he also has taught college: World Religions, Ethics, Biblical Hebrew and Biblical Greek (recently at College of Idaho). He has been a freelance researcher, writer, and editor for Stephen Ministries. His sermons and articles have appeared in *Interpretation*, *Pulpit Digest*, *Preaching*, *Lectionary Homiletics*, *Emphasis*, and *Preaching the Great Texts*. He wrote a year-long online column: "In The Original: Insights from Greek and Hebrew for the Lectionary Passages." His books include: *Gospel Subplots: Story Sermons of God's Grace*; *Toward Easter and Beyond*; *Scenes of Glory: Subplots of God's Long Story*; and *To the Cross and Beyond and Beyond: Cycle A Sermons for Lent and Easter*.

Sandra Herrmann is a retired pastor and popular teacher in the Wisconsin Conference of the United Methodist Church. She is a poet and the author of *Ambassadors of Hope* (CSS). She has been published in *alive now!*, a magazine of spirituality of the UMC, *Emphasis* magazine for pastors, and currently writes monthly for *StoryShare*. She is working on a book exploring the Christian iconography of the *Harry Potter* series.

Keith Hewitt is the author of two volumes of *NaTiVity Dramas: Nontraditional Christmas Plays for All Ages* (CSS). He is a local pastor, co-youth leader, an occasional speaker at Christmas events, and former Sunday school teacher at Wilmot United Methodist Church in Wilmot, Wisconsin. He lives in southeastern Wisconsin with his wife, two children, and assorted dogs and cats.

Craig Kelly is an office assistant living in Lima, Ohio. He received his B.A. from the University of Saskatchewan in 2002. He and his wife, Beth, are actively involved in their church, working both in their church's children's ministry as well as working with low-income youth in their neighborhood. Craig enjoys reading, music, hiking, biking, and indulging in old sci-fi movies.

W. Lamar Massingill, a former Southern Baptist pastor, now serves as Religion Editor for the *Magnolia Gazette* and as a guest columnist for the *United Methodist Advocate*. Massingill is the author of two books, *New Eyes: A Spirituality of Identity Formation* and *Soul Places*, and he has lectured widely on the interaction between religion and psychology. He is a graduate of William Carey University and New Orleans Baptist Theological Seminary.

C. David McKirachan is pastor of the Presbyterian Church at Shrewsbury in central New Jersey. He also teaches at Monmouth University. McKirachan is the author of *I Happened Upon a Miracle* and *A Year of Wonder* (Westminster John Knox).

Frank Ramirez has served as a pastor for nearly 30 years in Church of the Brethren congregations in Los Angeles, California; Elkhart, Indiana; and Everett, Pennsylvania. A graduate of LaVerne College and Bethany Theological Seminary, Ramirez is the author of numerous books, articles, and short stories. His CSS titles include *Partners in Healing*, *He Took a Towel*, *The Bee Attitudes*, and three volumes of *Lectionary Worship Aids*.

Argile Smith is vice president for advancement at William Carey University in Hattiesburg, Mississippi. He previously served at New Orleans Baptist Theological Seminary

(NOBTS) as a preaching professor, chairman of the Division of Pastoral Ministries, and director of the communications center. While at NOTBS, Smith regularly hosted the *Gateway to Truth* program on the FamilyNet television network. He has also been the pastor of several congregations in Louisiana and Mississippi. Smith's articles have been widely published in church periodicals, and he is the author or editor of four books.

Peter Andrew Smith is an ordained minister in the United Church of Canada currently serving St. James United Church in Antigonish, Nova Scotia. He is the author of *All Things Are Ready* (CSS), a book of lectionary-based communion prayers. He is also the author of a number of stories and articles, which can be found listed at www.peterandrewsmith.com.

The Rt. Rev. John S. Smylie, Bishop of Wyoming, previously served as the rector of St. Mark's Episcopal Church in Casper, Wyoming, and as the dean of the Cathedral of St. John the Evangelist in Spokane, Washington. He is a published author and storyteller as well as a singer-songwriter. Smylie recently completed *Grace for Today*, a collection of 25 stories that explores how grace, loss, and restoration are part of the same fabric.

John Sumwalt is the pastor of Our Lord's United Methodist Church in New Berlin, Wisconsin, and a noted storyteller. He is the author of nine books, including the acclaimed *Vision Stories* series and *How to Preach the Miracles: Why People Don't Believe Them and What You Can Do About It*. John and his wife Jo Perry-Sumwalt served for three years as the co-editors of *StoryShare*. A graduate of the University of Wisconsin-Madison and the University of Dubuque

Theological Seminary (UDTS), Sumwalt received the Herbert Manning Jr. award for parish ministry from UDTS in 1997.

Larry Winebrenner graduated from Garrett Biblical Institute (now Garrett-Evangelical Theological Seminary) over fifty years ago. He has been published in such varied publications as *The Christian Advocate*, *Games* magazine, and *Numismatic News*. He has been a contributor to StoryShare for a number of years. Larry served churches in Georgia, the Florida Keys, Indiana, and Wisconsin before returning to Miami, Florida, to teach at Miami-Dade College. He was an essential part of seeing the institution grow from a few classes held in a converted chicken coop to becoming the largest college in the United States of America. He now holds the title Professor Emeritus from that institution.

www.ingramcontent.com/pod-product-compliance
Lightning Source LLC
Chambersburg PA
CBHW070752100426
42742CB00012B/2112